The Rebirth of Patriotism
&
Old-fashioned Values

by Mike Radford

D1073024

Mike Radford
PO Box 7713
Branson, MO 65616
or call 800-745-5311

Visit our website at: www.mikeradford.com

Cover designed by Mike Sears

Printed in the United States of America
R.J. Communications, New York, NY

Library of Congress Cataloging-in-Publication Data
Radford, Mike
The Rebirth of Patriotism & Old Fashioned Values
Library of Congress
ISBN - # 0-9705766-0-9

Table of Contents

"In God We Trust"

About The Author
Michael J. Radford
www.mikeradford.com

CNN's Larry King says, "Mike is one of the most talented communicators in America today... a real pro." Mike is an outstanding speaker and talent, including many years working on the lot at ABC Television, and producer and sportscaster. It was during the 1982 annual Broadcasters Convention in Palm Springs when Mike convinced his friend Larry King his radio show would be successful if placed on the "new" cable network CNN. The rest is history.

A former shortstop with the Kansas City Royals, Mike laughs whenever asked, "How long did you play?" His response, "It was a very short stop! About 5 minutes!" After baseball his career naturally led to sportscasting. Later Mike produced and hosted programs on nearly every major network.

For nearly ten years Mike was a special advisor in the both the Reagan & Bush Administrations working with the Justice Department, The D.E.A., The National Fitness Foundation and The President's Council on Physical Fitness & Sports under the late NFL Head Coach, George H. Allen.

In addition to performing his hit stage show, the Remember When Show in Branson, Mo., Mike speaks passionately at military reunions and corporate conventions. Mike is a popular motivational speaker having shared the platform with Nancy Reagan, General Chuck Yeager, Jack LaLanne and his personal hero, the late Mickey Mantle. His fourth book, "Remember When Again" was published in '98 with NBC TV's Willard Scott writing the introduction.

Mike was appointed by Senator Bob Dole's office and The WW II Memorial Foundation in Washington D.C. to spearhead Branson's fund-raising efforts toward the memorial. In the summer of 2000, The Radisson Hotel in Branson, MO opened Mike Radford's Remember When Veterans Cafe dedicated to honoring the servicemen and women of all generations.

Mike has also joined General Colin Powell's efforts raising funds for America's Promise, a mentoring program for America's young people.

Other books by Mike Radford

"The Team of Champions" 1978 (out of print)
"How To Create Championship Vision" Kendall-Hunt 1994
"Remember When" 1997 (out of print)
Remember When Again" 1998

Acknowledgements

This is my fifth book. With each one there are so many people you must thank, for without their encouragement and help the work would never get completed. And like so many other authors, I pray I haven't forgotten anyone. My dear Mother Violet, kind, loving and the joy you give is so great. My step-father Gerald, thanks for all you have done for me. To my "adopted" brother Tim Rogers, words can not convey the depth of my respect and love for him. MSgt. Tony & Judy Gallagher, US Army (ret) my theatre manager affectionately called, "The Drill Sergeant." My manager in New York, Ben Carrizzo who taught me patience, patience and patience. Our old-fashioned "handshake" contract bound us together tighter than any piece of legal composition. Singer/songwriter Jimmie Rodgers entered my life in the '50s when I first heard "Honeycomb," and "Kisses Sweeter Than Wine." Now, Shari and I find ourselves included in his "family," we love you. Love too for our Branson "Mommie" Helen and Don Griffith for your ecouragement and keeping me focused, Avis Gutz, Commander Arnold Dominguez, Dr. Bob & Irene Barels and Col. Groninger (SR-71 pilot) & Lynn. Thanks to John & Vicki Allen-true friends always. Paul and Ann Bluto for building The Remember When Theatre for us. Amazing friends, Tony and Francine Orlando—when you called my show "The Best in Branson," you gave us the highest honor.

Dr. Jerry Davis, President of College of The Ozarks for your patriotic leadership. Thanks to Col. Bob Patrick and The W.W.II Memorial Foundation for asking me to spearhead Branson's fundraising. Thank you also, Senator Bob Dole and Jerry Luedke, two of my heroes. Chuck & Mary Schantag for their tireless work for POW/MIAs. To my colleagues Gayle Kirchner and Linda Ward, thanks for all you do. The Smiley family who stand tall as Americans. Richard Clark & Sue Ann O'Neal. Love to George and Esther Manning, and Dorlee St. John. To all my colleagues at the Branson Radisson Hotel, thanks to Tammy Johnson & Bill Weimar for allowing me to team up with you. Special kudos to Glenn Witzenburg and Fred Hoppe for building The Veterans Memorial Museum to Branson. Mike and Sandy Ramirez, airplane partners and dearest of pals. The Lowthers and Mary Eisenhower. Thanks for the great stories of your grandfather. Bob and Doris Knott, the best in-laws ever. My kids, Melissa, Andy and Kristin, all passionate lovers of freedom. Finally, Shawn McKinley, Ray Warren and Paul Salley the professional web guru's I most admire. Lastly, a personal thank you to my Lord and Savior, Jesus Christ, for without Him we'd all be toast.

Dedication

In every generation, role models have influenced and shaped the lives of countless people. This book is dedicated to a women who was known as a southern Belle, a true "Lady" with a gentle soul. Everyone called her "Aunt Virginia" a powerful example of Christian virtue and gentility. And her adoring husband, "Uncle Bob" who was a true patriot and veteran of WWII. Their lives are a testimont of old-fashioned values and virtue.

This book is lovingly dedicated to the memory of Robert and Virginia Abernathy Trundle from Ringgold, Georgia.

Robert & Virginia Trundle

The Angel on the Highway

It all began as I drove along I-94 returning from a speaking engagement at the Capitol in Madison, Wisconsin. I noticed a van ahead of me in the slow lane. As I drew closer, I could see words on the spare tire cover attached to the back of the vehicle. As I read the words goose bumps tightened on my skin:

"The Men and women who served and died for our country must NEVER be forgotten."

Chills began to crawl up my back. I pushed on the accelerator and pulled alongside the driver's door ... an elderly man sat behind the wheel ... obviously a veteran, I smiled and gave a thumbs-up gesture and began to pull ahead. Suddenly the old man began honking his horn, accelerating, until our cars were once again side-by-side.

What happened next was the turning point, the exact moment that changed my life forever. The white-haired veteran rolled down his window, stuck his arm out, pointed toward heaven then covered his heart and pointed directly back at me. At that moment I knew I had to create a show that would honor his generation, the generation that literally saved the world during WWII.

Over the past six years in Branson, dozens of pastors, priests and rabbis have seen my show or heard me speak of this experience. All agree that no one has seen this van or the white-haired man. They said it was an Angel put there to inspire me to write The Remember When Show and to spread old-fashioned patriotism honoring God, Family and Country.

A Special Thank You

Nearly twelve years ago God blessed me. It happened when yours truly thought single-parenthood and loneliness was my destiny. After much prayer, in fact very specific prayer, God brought a woman into my life who has become my best friend and wife, Shari. She continues to amaze me with her joyful and happy spirit. Her charming ways and spontaneous laughter enchant all who meet her. Thank you for the love you give me and so unselfishly share with others. You are my "dream-girl," — my life.

The Battle Cry of our Founders:
"Don't Tread On Me!"

A Wake-Up Call

We are in a war, a battle for the very survival of The United States of America. A war that if lost, will see the sovereignty of our nation handed to people who are secretly maneuvering to place our country under the control of the "Global village," or as others call it, The United Nations. Our Founders never intended for our sons and daughters to fight or be "peace-keepers" under the control of foreign governments. That is NOT what sovereignty means, and when a soldier is commanded to take action from officers of foreign Armies, that too flies in the face of the military pledge of defending our nation against all enemies, foreign and domestic. If we surrender our freedom and control to foreign military powers, we, in our lifetime will watch as our sons and daughters die under U.N. flags in battles around the world. What will we tell their widows and children? Will it be enough to say their daddy or mommie died protecting a piece of land that has been the scene of ethnic cleansing for thousands of years? Will they understand why our nation sent them to some far off land to die, defending causes we know nothing about? There is only one way for God loving men and women to prevent this careless absurdity from taking place. We must become reborn in the passionate belief that we are Americans, "One Nation under God" and will not waiver from the ideals our founding fathers set forth in our Bill of Rights and the Constitution of The United States.

One of the things I want this book to accomplish is to renew your sense of American pride, because with a renewed sense of who we are, comes a "rebirth" of those values most Americans hold dear. It is critically important we do this and teach our youngsters that living in The United States of America is a God-given privilege, not just a birthright. We can not take for granted, or assume the blessings of liberty will automatically be transferred from one generation to the next. We must teach our children and grandchildren the price others have paid so they can enjoy gifts of liberty and the true meaning of freedom that we have in our country today.

Too many of us have forgotten there are over 8,200 servicemen M.I.A. (Missing in Action) in Korea, nearly 3,000 in Vietnam and southeast Asia. We must not forget them! Don't wait until Veterans Day, the 4th of July, or Memorial Day to think of these abandoned patriots. When you see a veteran who was lucky enough to come home, shake their hand. Thank them for serving our country and doing their part to keep our republic free. This gesture will be something they never expected and their reactions will be something you will never forget. No, freedom is not free. Millions have died so you and I could delight in freedom's blessings ... it is time for a "Rebirth of Patriotism," and America needs your help to make this happen.

A City of Destiny

When I thought about writing this book, my first thoughts were "how" to embark upon the subject for which I feel such passion. This, at a time when most Americans aren't, or at best apathetic about national politics and concerns. Some authors write the ending first, then "flesh it out" as its' called. So, before we get going, I thought it would be fun to share some of my personal thoughts about living and working in Branson, Missouri. My wife Shari and I feel we are blessed to be living in the middle of the Ozark Mountains where millions of visitors come to experience America like it used to be.

Branson was originally known as a world-class fishing Mecca, but all that has changed since millions of theatre goers have discovered Branson, catapulting our little city into stardom. Branson has carved out a rather sizable and unique niche in the tourism industry. It is a place where good old-fashioned American values can still be found and a Mecca for people who still remove their hats when the National Anthem is played and bow their heads before each meal. Branson represents a time when family came first and a man's handshake was his bond. Yes, Branson is a page torn from the past, a Rockwell painting of Americana, because life is still the way it used to be. When you come here you will feel it. This feeling of patriotic destiny isn't something that evolved here. Just as with people, cities have destinies too. Remember the incredible story of Cory ten Boom? She was the Dutch woman who gave refuge to thousands of Jewish people trying to outrun the Nazi storm-troopers. Her many books became best sellers, in fact "The Hiding Place" became a major motion picture. Her popularity as an author naturally led to celebrity status. She was an engaging orator with the ability to mesmerize audiences with her magnetic storytelling. One day, I think in the early 60s while on a speaking tour, Mrs. ten Boom chartered a private airplane to take her from city to city. While relaxing inside the cabin she suddenly felt The Lord's presence. She quickly leaned forward and asked the pilot to pinpoint on his map their location. He immediately pointed to a little area just south of Springfield, Missouri. She asked her pilot the exact name of the city they were directly above. "Branson, and Lake Taneycomo," he said. "The Lord is going to use Branson for His work," she said, "He just spoke to my heart and said this is an anointed land and He will use this area to fulfill His glory on earth." What else can explain the incredible growth and dynamics of a sleepy little town nestled in the Ozarks. I believe God is using Branson for His purposes and the best is yet to be seen. One way to describe Branson's outreach is in this analogy: If you throw a rock into a pond, we see the ripples expand and flow out from where the rock first splashed. The "Branson effect" is exactly the same principle. The people who come here experience a city that is still functioning with old-fashioned values. Patriotism is proudly promoted here and those aspects of life are the "pebbles" we throw into the preverbal pond. Our ripples widen too, they expand from Canada to Mexico and from the east coast to the west coast. The Branson way of life continues spreading across the land. Yes, Branson is like a beacon in a dark night drawing ships to the safety and warmth of their home-port. Communities want what Branson has. When visitors come here, they literally feel a rush of energy, a breath of fresh air, some call it. They are drawn here and they don't even know why. Ask any of the people who have quit jobs and moved here. They will say they were led by unseen forces inside their hearts, further proof that a spiritual hand does indeed guide us. Cory ten Boom's vision is confirmed everyday, because Branson is definately a part of God's plan for our nation's renewal.

Bear in mind, my foremost objective throughout this book is to inspire you, to light a fire inside your heart that will motivate you to want to make your town a better place. I want you to look deep inside and find the roots of your patriotism, to discover hidden passions that will help propel you to a higher level of commitment to God, family and country.

Enjoy the journey you are about to take. Share the inspiration with those you love and together we can chart the course of America's future. Together we can make a difference.

The American G.I.

When I was still a little kid, my grandma Harriet loved taking me to watch parades. Grandma looked forward to standing along the curb with her little "Mikey." I remember vividly seeing all the veterans marching, heads held high, chests stuck out. I'd watch grandma's eyes fill with tears, then fall across her rosy cheeks as the boys marched down the main street carrying flags and rifles. Patriotism was big back then. "Why are you crying?" I asked her. "I'm proud of our boys Mikey, I'm so proud of these boys." She'd say. Now forty-odd years later her voice rings loud in my heart. Isn't it time for kids today to learn and feel that old-fashioned pride? To discover the G.I. and learn of the sacrifices and heroics they displayed during the days of their youth. The American G.I. has become an unsung hero in our time and it is time our nation salute and celebrate their countless contributions.

In 1999, Time Magazine prepared a list of the 10 most influential people of the last century. They named "the American G.I." the most influential "person" of The Twenty-first Century. When the honor was announced, General Colin Powell gave the introduction to the award:

Colin Powell's Tribute to the American G.I.

As Chairman of the Joint Chiefs of Staff, I referred to the men and women of the armed forces as "G.I.s." It got me in trouble

18

with some of my colleagues at the time. Several years earlier, the Army had officially excised the term as an unfavorable characterization derived from the designation "government issue." Sailors and Marines wanted to be known as sailors and Marines. Airmen, notwithstanding their origins as a rib of the Army, wished to be called simply airmen. Collectively, they were blandly referred to as "service members."

I persisted in using G.I.s and found I was in good company. Newspapers and television shows used it all the time. The most famous and successful government education program was known as the G.I. Bill, and it still uses that title for a newer generation of veterans. When you added one of the most common boy's names to it, you got G.I. Joe, and the name of the most popular boy's toy ever, the G.I. Joe action figure. And let's not forget G.I. Jane.

G.I. is a World War II term that two generations later continues to conjure up the warmest and proudest memories of a noble war that pitted pure good against pure evil and good triumphed.

The victors in that war were the American G.I.s, the Willies and Joes, the farmer from Iowa and the steelworker from Pittsburgh who stepped off a landing craft into the hell of Omaha Beach. The G.I. was the wisecracking kid Marine from Brooklyn who clawed his way up a deadly hill on a Pacific island.

He was a black fighter pilot escorting white bomber pilots over Italy and Germany, proving that skin color had nothing to do with skill or courage. He was a native Japanese-American infantryman released from his own country's concentration camp to join the fight.

She was a nurse relieving the agony of a dying teenager. He was a petty officer standing on the edge of a heaving aircraft carrier with two signal paddles in his hands, helping guide a dive-bomber pilot back onto the deck. They were America.

They reflected our diverse origins. They were the embodiment of the American spirit of courage and dedication. They were truly a "people's army," going forth on a crusade to save democracy and freedom, to defeat tyrants, to save oppressed peoples and to make their families proud of them. They were the Private Ryans, and they stood firm in the thin red line.

For most of those G.I.s, World War II was the adventure of their lifetime. Nothing they would ever do in the future would match their experiences as the warriors of democracy, saving the world from its own insanity. You can still see them in every Fourth of July color guard, their gait faltering but ever proud.

Their forebears went by other names: doughboys, Yanks, buffalo soldiers, Johnny Reb, Rough-Riders. But "G.I." will be forever lodged in the consciousness of our nation to apply to all of them. The G.I. carried the value system of the American people. The G.I.s were the surest guarantee of America's commitment.

For more than 200 years, they answered the call to fight the nation's battles. They never went forth as mercenaries on the road to conquest.

They went forth as reluctant warriors, as citizen soldiers. They were as gentle in victory as they were vicious in battle.

I've had survivors of Nazi concentration camps tell me of the joy they experienced as the G.I.s liberated them: America had arrived!

I've had a wealthy Japanese businessman come into my office and tell me what it was like for him as a child in 1945 to await the arrival of the dreaded American beasts, and instead meet a smiling G.I. who gave him a Hershey bar. In thanks, the businessman was donating a large sum of money to the USO. After thanking him, I gave him as a souvenir a Hershey bar I had autographed. He took it and began to cry. The 20th century can be called many things, but it was most certainly a century of war. The American G.I.s helped defeat fascism and communism.

They came home in triumph from the ferocious battlefields of World Wars I and II. In Korea and Vietnam they fought just as bravely as their predecessors, but no triumphant receptions awaited them at home. They soldiered on through the twilight struggles of the cold war and showed what they were capable of in Desert Storm. The American people took them into their hearts again.

In this century hundreds of thousands of G.I.s died to bring to the beginning of the 21st century the victory of democracy as the ascendant political system on the face of the earth. The G.I.s were willing to travel far away and give their lives, if necessary, to secure the rights and freedoms of others. Only a nation such as our's, based on a firm moral foundation, could make such a request of its citizens. And the G.I.s wanted nothing more than to get the job done and then return home safely. All they asked for in repayment from those they freed was the opportunity to help them become part of the world of democracy-and just enough land to bury their fallen comrades, beneath simple white crosses and Stars of David.

The volunteer G.I.s of today stand watch in Korea, the Persian Gulf, Europe and the dangerous terrain of the Balkans. We must never see them as mere hirelings, off in a corner of our society. They are our best, and we owe them our full support and our sincerest thanks. As this century closes, we look back to identify the great leaders and personalities of the past 100 years. We do so in a world still troubled, but full of promise. That promise was gained by the young men and women of America who fought and died for freedom. Near the top of any listing of the most important people of the 20th century must stand, in singular honor, the American G.I. [1]

General Colin Powell, former Chairman of the Joint Chiefs of Staff, is now Chairman of America's Promise and destined for high positions in The White House. His words always inspire and his long and distinguished military career, dedication to patriotism makes him the role model every generation should revere. We salute him.

50s Role Models

After performing our "Remember When Show" one day, I had the chance to chat with a little lady from Ohio. I asked what she would change in American culture today. Her answer was swift and to the point— She wished today's kids could see the same clean and wholesome movies she grew-up watching back in the 40s and 50s. I couldn't agree more. Back then, our role models never got arrested, and moms and dads across the U.S.A. never worried about their kids on week-ends because the Saturday matinee was the coolest place to be and the theatre ushers and staff always cared for the kids and made sure everyone was OK. Yep, when I was growing up in the '50s, there were two people most kids pretended to "be." We'd jump on our stick ponies and ride out behind the barn to look for those make-believe bad guys we knew were always hiding along the trail, waiting to bushwhack us little buckaroos. The two movie stars we "became" were Roy Rogers & Dale Evans. I loved Roy & Dale with all my heart, and I still do! They taught us right from wrong and always defended the helpless. Yes, I feel sad for kids today, because they don't have the kind of role models we did back when we were young.

America needs people like them more than ever before because they stood for everything that was good and unsoiled in our nation. Here's a simple but poignant example of Roy Rogers philosophy of teaching us kids right from wrong:

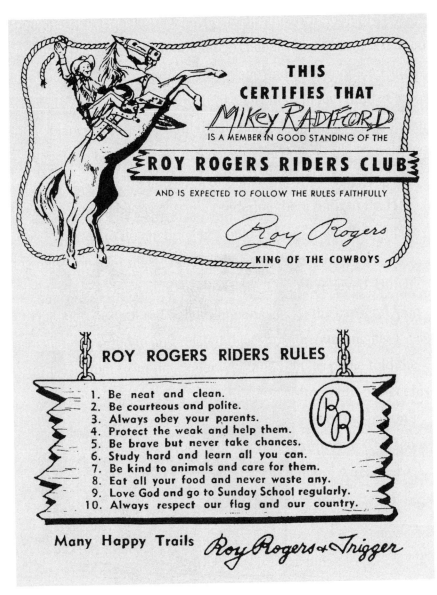

Simple common sense rules that built character.

In 1994 Roy Roger's family gave Mike permission to create his version.

A man from Michigan just last week told me about how he patterned his life after one of his childhood heroes and went on to finish medical school. His hero— was his dad. So you see not all our heroes were up on the silver screen or playing in Yankee Stadium... no... the real heroes are the moms and dads, the grandpas and grandmas who show us how to live with dignity and grace. It's their examples of old-fashioned patriotism and polite manners that we need to teach today's youth. That's why our old-time role models were so good for us, there was no gray area, we all knew the difference between right and wrong. Today the lines are so blurry a kid can't figure out what is right and wrong. Back in the 30s, 40s & 50s, when the movie was over and "THE END" came on the screen it was the guy in the white hat who always got the girl, while the bad guys in the black hats always went to the pokey. Oh if only it could be that simple again.

Thinking back to those days, I remember how patriotic our teachers were. In February, or during a president's birthday our classroom assignments always revolved around essays and book reports about the presidents. Remember cutting silhouettes of their heads and stapling them all around the classroom? When I was a kid in the 50s, we always celebrated Dwight David Eisenhower's birthday in October. His birthday was easy for me to remember because many important things happened on that day, the fourteenth of October. It was President Eisenhower's birthday, it was the day Chuck Yeager became the first pilot to brake the sound barrier and live to tell about it. Then on October 14th, 1964 a young United States Marine, Lt. Billy Mills shocked the Olympic world winning the Gold Medal in the 10,000 meters. Oh, and one other great event took place on October 14th, just like Chuck Yeager, I too "broke" the sound barrier! It's the day I was born in 1946!

My first memories of patriotic celebration began when I was around five-years-old. My grandpa Mitch was a veteran of W.W.I and I remember sitting on his knee as he tried to teach me to speak the very limited Italian and French he'd picked up while fighting in the trenches in Europe. Once in a while I would see his eyes seem to lose focus as his mind wondered somewhere. The normal relaxed features of his face would often harden then with a shake of his head, he would return back to me sitting on his leg. Back then our family was mostly Democrats. Even for a youngster like me, it was fun watching Harry Truman occasionally rant and rave on grandpa's old black and white television set. Grandpa used to tell me to watch President Truman, to learn from him and be honest and always say what's on my mind. I guess without knowing it, Mr. Truman became an early influence on my character too. "Give'm Hell Harry!" Grandpa Mitch would shout, fist shaking high above his head. Whenever he got too upset about something on television, Grandma Harriet would yell from out in the kitchen, "Now calm down Mitch! You mustn't talk like that in front of Mikey!" She'd then return to her kitchenly duties whistling her happy tunes. Yes, school days were different then. History was something all our teachers seemed to be interested in back when I was a kid. We were all proud Americans then. Do you think all that patriotism could be traced back to the positive role models, the likes of Eisenhower, Roy Rogers, Gene Autry and even Sky King? Makes you think, doesn't it.

Teachers

When I was still little "Mikey" there were two teachers that really stand out in my memory. One is a cheerful, but very large woman, Mrs. Sparks, the other came along many years later, his name was Dr. Weatherspoon. Let me tell you a little about Mrs. Sparks. As with every first day of school, my third grade was particularly stressful. It was a mixture of excitement and hopeful anticipation. "Oh, please God, make her nice, make her like me!" I'd pray. The third grade was going to be a major turning point in my life. It would be the last time I would attend Olive View School in Corning, California, the final months playing with my buddy Earl Benning, who would soon move to Edinburgh, Scotland, and unknown to me, we too would pack our things in a moving van and head down Highway 99 to live in Sacramento. But in the last few months under Mrs. Sparks tutelage, two major lessons were about to be learned. We were making Christmas ornaments that day, remember those red and green strips of construction paper cut into thin pieces, then slapped together with white paste. It was my assignment to use the paper cutter and with precision and great care, I returned to my work area with a stack of soon-to-be rings to add to the paper chain destined to adorn our class Christmas tree. "Mikey!" I heard Mrs. Sparks say, "Come over here right now." Her usual soft and gentle approach to education had suddenly taken on a serious tone. I shuffled past my little buddies and looked up at my teacher who was obviously not pleased with something I had done. "Yes, Mrs. Sparks," I said sheepishly. I stood next to her with the top of my head barely reaching her waistline. She pointed to the paper cutter sitting atop the work-table. "What's this?" She asked. "A paper cutter." I shyly replied. "And just what might happen if someone were to put their little fingers under that blade that you've left up?" I got the point. Funny how something as trivial as this paper cutter sticks so vividly in my mind. To this day I never leave a paper cutter with the blade not securely fastened as Mrs. Sparks taught me. My wife, Shari thinks its funny how I'm obsessed with paper cutters being closed. But you know what? I guess the lesson here is our teachers really do have a huge impact on shaping our lives. Thank you Mrs. Sparks, not only for the paper cutter lesson but all the kindness you gave to your students.

Years later another teacher would impact my life and help create the passion I have for American history and patriotism. His name was Dr. Weatherspoon. In 1965, I had the honor of attending his class during my first semester at American River College in Carmichael, California. Dr. Weatherspoon was blind, or should I say "sightless" because this man "saw" more history and reached his students in such dynamic ways. We all had teachers who seemed to go through the duties of their job as teachers, but lack any passion in what they do. Professor Weatherspoon was different. This man was enthusiastic. This was an educator.

The morning sunlight streamed into the lecture hall as we prepared for the first of many griping lectures by a professor who was widely known as one of the college's best. We were studying The American Revolution. Professor Weatherspoon quietly entered the large room, his German Shepherd guide dog leading the way across the stage. The elegant and graceful canine carefully guided his master to the podium. The class sat in silence awaiting our first day instructions. The professor stood erect, hands resting on each side of the lectern. We continued to sit in polite silence, seconds ticking away until each of us became a little uncomfortable. Minutes passed, some students began to squirm in their seats as the Professor stood silent, staring out into the darkness straight ahead of him. Then with the swiftness of a lightening bolt he shouted, "General Cornwalis and the red coats began to charge the unprepared minutemen!" "Gun powder flashed as muskets spewed their deadly balls of lead whose projectiles ripped flesh and shattered the bones of the enemy!" This man was a genius at communication. From the moment he spoke he had every student in the palm of his hand. His style and flair for the dramatic, would forever influence me. It was this teacher, more than any other helped shape my love for history.

What is the lesson here? Be enthusiastic. Show the world you are passionate about something...then people will listen to what you have to say.

Authors Note: Get your tissues ready for these stories.

"All Good Things"

by Sister Helen P. Mrosia

He was in the very first Third grade class I taught at Saint Mary's School in Morris, Minnesota. All 34 of my students were dear to me, but Mark Eklund was one in a million. He was very neat, but had that happy-to-be-alive attitude that made even his occasional mischievousness delightful.

Mark talked incessantly. I had to remind him again and again that talking without permission was not acceptable. What impressed me so much though, was his sincere response every time I had to correct him for misbehaving - "Thank you for correcting me, Sister!" I didn't know what to make of it at first, but before long I became accustomed to hearing it many times a day.

One morning my patience was growing thin when Mark talked once too often, and then I made a 'novice'-teacher's mistake. I looked at him and said, "If you say one more word, I'm going to tape your mouth shut!"

It wasn't ten seconds later when another student blurted out, "Mark is talking again!" I had to act. I remember the scene as if it occurred this morning. I walked to my desk, very deliberately opened my drawer and took out a roll of masking tape and without saying a word proceeded to Mark's desk, tore off two pieces and made a big X over his mouth. I then returned to the front of the room. As I glanced back at Mark to see how he was doing, he winked at me! That did it. I started laughing as the whole class cheered as I walked back to Mark and removed the tape. I shrugged my shoulders and his first words were, "Thank you for correcting me Sister!"

At the end of the year I was asked to teach junior high-math. The years flew by and before I knew it Mark was in my classroom again. He was more handsome than ever and just as polite. Since he had to listen carefully to my instructions in the "New Math" he did not talk as much in the ninth grade as he had in the third.

One Friday, things just didn't feel right in the classroom. The students were all depressed and I sensed their frustration. I had to stop this crankiness before it got out of hand, so I asked them to list the names of the other students in the room and list all the things they liked about each other.

It took the remainder of the class period to finish the assignment, and as the students left the room, each handed me the papers. Mark said, "Thank you for teaching me Sister. Have a good weekend."

That Saturday, I wrote down the name of each student on a separate sheet of paper and listed what everyone else had said about that individual. On Monday I gave each student his or her list. Before long, the entire class was smiling. "Really?" I heard whispered. "I never knew that meant anything to anyone." Another said, "I didn't know others like me so much!"

No one ever mentioned those papers in class again. I never knew if they discussed them after class or with their parents, but it didn't matter. The exercise had accomplished its purpose. The students were happy with themselves and one another again.

That group of students moved on. Several years later, after I returned from a vacation, my parents met me at the airport. As we were driving home, Mother asked me the usual questions about the trip - the weather, my experiences in general. There was a light lull in the conversation when Mother gave Dad a sideways glance and simply said, "Dad?" My father cleared his throat as he usually did before something important. "The Eklunds called last night," he began. "Really?" I said. "I haven't heard from them in years. I wonder how Mark is doing."

Dad responded quietly. "Mark was killed in Vietnam last week," he said. "The funeral is tomorrow and his parents would like it if you could attend." To this day I can still point to the exact spot on I-494 where my Dad told me about Mark.

I had never seen a serviceman in a military coffin before. Dear Mark looked so handsome, so mature. All I could think at that moment was, Mark, I would give all the masking tape in the world if only you would talk to me!

The Church was packed with Mark's friends. Why did it have to rain on the day of the funeral? It was difficult enough at the grave-side. The pastor said the usual prayers, and the bugler played Taps. One by one, those who loved Mark took a last walk by the coffin and sprinkled it with Holy water. I was the last one to bless the coffin. As I stood there, one of the soldiers who had acted as pallbearer came up to me and asked, "Were you Mark's math teacher?" I nodded as I continued to stare at the coffin. "Mark talked about you all the time," he said.

After the funeral, most of Mark's former classmates headed to Chuck's farmhouse for lunch. Mark's mother and father were there, obviously waiting for me. "We want you to know something," his father said, taking a wallet out of his pocket. "They found this on Mark when he was killed. We thought you might recognize it." Opening the billfold, he carefully removed two worn pieces of notebook paper that had obviously been taped, folded and refolded many times. I knew without looking that the papers were the ones on which I had listed all the good things each of Mark's classmates had said about him. "Thank you so much for doing that," Mark's mother said. "As you can see, Mark treasured it." Mark's classmates started to gather around us. Charlie smiled rather sheepishly and said, "I still have my list. It's in the top drawer of my desk." Chuck's wife said, "Chuck asked me to put this in our wedding album." I have mine too," Marilyn said. "It's in my diary." Then Vicki, another classmate reached into her pocketbook, took out her wallet and showed her worn and frazzled list to the group. "I carry this with me at all times," Vicki said without batting an eyelash. "I think we all saved our lists." That's when I finally sat down and began to cry. I cried for Mark and for all his friends who would never see him again. (Originally sent by, Dorothy Watson, Columbia, MO) [3].

Here's another story I received, once again the author is unknown:

I had a very special teacher in high school many years ago whose husband unexpectedly died of a heart attack. About a week after his death, she shared some of her insight with a classroom of students. As the late afternoon sunlight came streaming in through the classroom windows, and the class was nearly over, she moved a few things aside on the edge of her desk and sat down. With a gentle look of reflection on her face, she paused and said, "Before class is over, I would like to share with all of you a thought that is unrelated to class, but which I feel is very important.

Each of us is put here on earth to learn, share, love, appreciate and give of ourselves. None of us knows when this fantastic experience will end. It can be taken away at any moment. Perhaps this is God's way of telling us that we must make the most out of every single day. Her eyes beginning to water, she went on, "So I would like you all to make me a promise. From now on, in route to school, or on your way home, you will find something beautiful to notice. It doesn't have to be something you see. It could be a scent of freshly baked bread wafting from an open window. It could be the sound of the breeze slightly rustling the leaves in the trees, or the way the morning light catches one autumn leaf as it falls gently to the ground. Please, look for these things and cherish them. For although it may sound trite to some, these things are the "essence" of life. The little things we are put here on earth to enjoy. The things we often take for granted. We must make it important to notice them, for at any time it can all be taken away."

The class was completely quiet. We all picked up our books and filed out of the room silently. That afternoon, I noticed more things on my way home from school than I had that whole semester. Every once in a while, I think of that teacher and remember what an impression she made on all of us, and I try to appreciate all of those things that sometimes we all overlook. Take notice of something special on your lunch hour or commute home today. Go barefoot. Or walk by the water at sunset. Stop on the way home and enjoy a double dip ice cream cone before dinner! For as we get older, it is not the things we did that we often regret, but the things we didn't do. 4.

Her name was Mrs. Thompson

(Author unknown)

As she stood in front of her 5th grade class on the very first day of school, she told the children a lie, no one would favored. Like most teachers, she looked at some students as impossible. There in the front row, slumped in his seat, was a little boy named Teddy Stoddard.

Mrs. Thompson had watched Teddy the year before and noticed that he didn't play well with the other children, that his clothes were messy and that he constantly needed a bath. And Teddy could be unpleasant. It got to the point where Mrs. Thompson would actually take delight in marking his papers with a broad red pen, making bold X's and then putting a big "F" at the top of his papers.

At the school where Mrs. Thompson taught, she was required to review each child's past records and she put Teddy's off until last. However, when she reviewed his file, she was in for a surprise.

Teddy's first grade teacher wrote, "Teddy is a bright child with a ready laugh. He does his work neatly and has good manners...he is a joy to be around."

His second grade teacher wrote, "Teddy is an excellent student, well liked by his classmates, but he is troubled because his mother has a terminal illness and life at home must be a struggle."

His third grade teacher wrote, "His mother's death had been

hard on him. He tries to do his best, but his father doesn't show much interest and his home life will soon affect him if some steps aren't taken." Teddy's fourth grade teacher wrote, "Teddy is withdrawn and doesn't show much interest in school. He doesn't have many friends and he sometimes sleeps in class." By now, Mrs. Thompson realized the problem and she was ashamed of herself. She felt even worse when her students brought her Christmas presents, wrapped in beautiful ribbons and bright paper, except for Teddy's. His present was clumsily wrapped in the heavy, brown paper that he got from a grocery bag. Mrs. Thompson took pains to open it in the middle of the other presents.

Some of the children started to laugh when she found a rhine-stone bracelet with some of the stones missing, and a bottle that was one quarter full of perfume. But she stifled the children's laughter when she exclaimed how pretty the bracelet was, putting it on, and dabbing some of the perfume on her wrist.

Teddy Stoddard stayed after school that day just long enough to say, "Mrs. Thompson, today you smelled just like my Mom used to." After the children left she cried for at least an hour. On that very day, she quit teaching reading, and writing, and arithmetic. Instead, she began to teach children.

Mrs. Thompson paid particular attention to Teddy. As she worked with him, his mind seemed to come alive. The more she encouraged him, the faster he responded. By the end of the year, Teddy had become one of the smartest children in the class and, despite her lie that she would love all the children the same, Teddy became one of her "teacher's pets." A year later, she found a note under her door, from Teddy, telling her that she was still the best teacher he ever had in his whole life.

Six years went by before she got another note from Teddy. He then wrote that he had finished high school, third in his class, and she was still the best teacher he ever had in his whole life. Four years after that, she got another letter saying that while things had been tough at times, he'd stayed in school, had stuck with it, and would soon graduate from college with the highest of honors.

He assured Mrs. Thompson that she was still the best and favorite teacher he ever had in his whole life. Then four more years passed and yet another letter came. This time he explained that after he got his bachelor's degree, he decided to go a little further. The letter explained that she was still the best and favorite teacher he ever had. But now his name was a little longer—the letter was signed,

Theodore F. Stoddard, MD.

The story doesn't end there. You see, there was yet another letter that spring. Teddy said he'd met this girl and was going to be married. He explained that his father had died a couple of years ago and he was wondering if Mrs. Thompson might agree to sit in the place at the wedding that was usually reserved for the mother of the groom. Of course, Mrs. Thompson did. And guess what? She wore that bracelet, the one with several rhinestones missing. And she made sure she was wearing the perfume that Teddy remembered his mother wearing on their last Christmas together. They hugged each other, and Dr. Stoddard whispered in Mrs. Thompson's ear, "Thank you Mrs. Thompson for believing in me. Thank you so much for making me feel important and showing me that I could make a difference." Mrs. Thompson, with tears in her eyes, whispered back. She said, "Teddy, you have it all wrong. You were the one who taught me that I could make a difference. I didn't know how to teach until I met you." [5.]

Warm someone's heart today . . . pass this story along to someone you care about. Remember, wherever you go, and whatever you do, you will have the opportunity to touch someone's heart and change their view of themselves and the world. Be a Mentor.

Teachers are the most important influences on our nation's young minds. They have enormous power to motivate us to greatness or destroy the dreamer. Lucky for me I had some pretty great people who shared my same passions for God, family and Country. In my opinion teachers are some of the greatest heroes in our society. They are the frontline role models for our nation's children.

What is a Veteran? What is a Patriot?

Shari and I are blessed to work in the entertainment industry and have our own theatre in Branson. Everyday we kind of pinch ourselves to see if it's all real because we are having so much fun performing and making people laugh, cry and "remember" the fun things in their lives. "The Remember When Show," known as a comedy with patriotism has continued to grow year after year and we know it's because of you. We know God is using us to do His work, and one of the hardest things to do is "get out of His way and let Him control whatever it is that He wants us to do!" Does that make sense? Anyway, when I began to consider what to write in regard to veterans and patriots, it became clear to me. Tell true stories of those men and women who epitomize the subject, people we know personally.

When we define the word veteran, Webster's says, "a person who served in the armed forces, an old experienced soldier." I have to laugh when I think about actually putting into print what my mind just flashed upon because some may not understand my sense of humor. But most of you have been to my show or heard my speeches so this is what caused me to chuckle when I first read the definition of a veteran. My first "vision" of a veteran as described (an old experienced soldier) was of a man whom I have grown to love, even though I respected him tremendously even before we met. The name of this "old experienced solder" is Robert Decatur, one of the famed "Tuskegee Airmen" from W.W. II. Trish Thompson, one of Branson's leading veteran advocates first introduced us and for that, Shari and I are forever grateful. Trish, a vivacious blonde affectionately called, "Trish-the-dish" by the famed flyers, is one of two women as honorary "Tuskegee Airman" the other, Ms. Lena Horne!

Now I must confess Bob Decatur is not that old, true he's in his seventies but he looks and carries himself with the stride of a man far younger. Getting to know Robert Decatur is one of our life's highest personal rewards. He's truly a patriot in every sense of the word. Bob grew up in Cleveland, Ohio and even played pro-fessional baseball in the old Negro National League. His team-mates were the likes of Jackie Robinson, Satchel Paige and Buck O'Neil. This is a man who always excelled in everything he did, and epitomizes the term "Excellence." As a young man who fin-ished College at twenty, he soon embarked on his military duty. And of course his military aspirations were to become a fighter pilot. Only one problem with that lofty goal, there were no black aviators, period. You must remember, during W.W. II this was lit-erally out of the question because "Negro's" were considered intellectually incapable of flying an airplane. But our friend, Bob Decatur is a man who dreams big dreams, then makes them happen, any obstacles in his way are just that, challenges to be defeated. As a young black airman cadet, he dreamed of flying P-51 Mustangs. He wanted to fight for his country, to defend his nation, a nation for which he would have given his life. What amazes me about Bob's patriotism, is his dedication to God, family and country, even though he lived in a nation where most of his race weren't allowed to vote, or drink water from the same public drinking fountains, or eat at the same restaurants. Thank God times changed. Recently at one of the national conventions for the "Tuskegge Airmen," General Colin Powell addressed the distinguished audience and said, "You are my heroes... it is upon your backs I rose to achieve my success. You are the wind beneath my wings!"

Bob Decatur's life is a rare testimony to the triumph of the human spirit to succeed beyond all odds and became the mentor for the likes of Colin Powell. Oh, there is one other achiever Bob inspired and called his friend, Dr. Martin Luther King. Bob remembers being with Dr. King the night before the assassination. He remembers saying, "Now Dr. King, don't you go down to Memphis and get yourself killed." It was the last thing they laughed about together.

Today, we look at the career of this amazing man and marvel at his accomplishments. If you have seen the movie "The Tuskegee Airmen," you might recall the scene where all the cadets had to retake an exam because one cadet scored a perfect 100% on a very difficult test. It was Bob Decatur. Another scene in the movie shows an airman developing engine problems and forced to land on a country road. Again it was Bob Decatur. Shari and I marvel at the fact we now call him our friend. Bob Decatur former WWII aviator, attorney, honored Judge, proud family man and father. Robert Decatur's life has been a blessing to his country, and a testimony to the triumph of a young man's dreams. His experiences are the "stuff" of legends. How many of us can say our friends were Jackie Robinson, Satchel Paige and Buck O'Neil? How many of us can say we became a Federal Judge, an Ambassador of the United States, and famed military aviator? We consider ourselves lucky to call him our friend.

"In 1998 we had another amazing man sitting in our audience in Branson. His name is Col. Ben Purcell and although I had no idea who he was, or what he did, this gentle man was to become one of our dearest friends, a man who is respected and loved by all who have the honor of knowing him. Ben has the distinction of being the highest ranking Army officer held as a P.O.W. in the Vietnam war.

He and his lovely wife Anne were passing through Branson on their way to the 25th anniversary of their release. In every sense of the word, these men are true patriots and real American Heroes. It is unfathomable to understand their experiences under the evil each POW suffered at the hands of the Communists who seemed to "enjoy" the pain they inflicted on our men. Col. Purcell was held in solitary confinement inside the famous "Hanoi Hilton." Today, his love of The Lord shines through his eyes and crosses his face in every easy smile he flashes. It was his faith in the Almighty that got him through it all. And he told us that many of his prison-mates died because they had no faith to carry them through. I asked him what he felt was the greatest blessing living as a free man. He looked toward the clear blue sky and in his easy Georgian style said, "The ability to rise in the morning and go for a walk. The liberty to stop and smell a flower, or the freedom to simply gaze into the blue skies of America and take in the deep sense of wonder. To feel the amazing joy that fills your heart knowing you are free!" He escaped several times but as luck would have it, recaptured again and again, until finally released when the war came to a close.

The last time they came to Branson, I asked Col. Purcell and his wife Anne to stand so I could introduce them to my audience. The crowd jumped to their feet and gave them a long, rousing standing ovation. His eyes filled with tears as the entire theatre stood in honor of this true patriot. Col. Purcell came up on the stage and shyly waved his "thanks" as is his style. The Purcells are not much on self-promotion. He slowly walked across the stage with that smile flashing across his face. I joined him in a bear-hug. Hugging was something he liked to do because affection was a luxury he hadn't experienced in the Communist prison. His eyes moist, he turned toward the crowd which now sat silently. "In 5 ½ years in solitary confinement I laughed only two times... and today seeing "The Remember When Show," and being with all of you... my cup runneth over." The sold-out crowd jumped to their feet again, cheering and applauding one of America's true patriots.

When you come to our theatre, just outside the entrance you will see the "Hall of Heroes." There are 100s of photographs and military memorabilia from every corner of our nation and Canada. One extraordinary display includes Col. Purcell's uniform, covered with medals and commendations. It is the very uniform he wore "Home" when our men were finally released from the hell they experienced in North Vietnam. Looking at Ben's uniform and the pictures taken only days before his release from captivity will touch you deeply. I hope you can come to Branson for the experience. If you are a veteran or would like to honor a family member, send me a photograph and I will add it to our second "Hall of Heroes" inside the Radisson Hotel. We have created our Veterans Cafe, R & R Bar and Canteen to honor our servicemen and women. Be sure to stop by and take a look at all the memorabilia. It will make you proud.

I receive thousands of patriotic pieces either in the mail or via the internet. This next story is one of the best — it paints a clear picture of the sacrifices our modern day patriots endure.

The Veterans: **Author unknown**

They are the ones who endure constant pain from a bullet fired fifty years ago... or smile back at the innocent child who stares at his missing limb...

She's the gal who raises her children to obey God's laws...then answers the call as her outfit is called to "Desert Storm" and finds herself sweltering in the Saudi desert...while 10,000 miles away her kids cry themselves to sleep while asking their daddy, "When's Mommy coming home?"

He's the POW who still screams in the night...and dreams of the day his MIA buddies will all come home.

She's the lady who checks out your groceries and always has a smile for you even though her headaches from an unknown sickness she picked up in Somalia...

She's the woman who tucks in her children at night, saying bedtime prayers with her kids as she silently prays for the children when blazing bullets made them orphans in Bosnia, Belfast and Boston...

He's the cop in your neighborhood who limps from the shrapnel in his leg, the bartender who pours you beer and remembers his buddies who were with him in Nam and a second later vaporized from a VC mortar... She's the nurse in Saigon who worked 20 hour days hoping against hope she could save every kid who came in, then sobbed herself to sleep every night when she couldn't.

He's a veteran named Jimmie Reese who, while with the

Yankees in '31 called Babe Ruth his "Roomie" and at the age of 92 smiled and said, "Never regret growing old ... for many are denied the privilege."

These and thousands more just like them are the true patriots... the heroes of our society. It's up to you and me to ensure their sacrifices and legacy live forever. Our nation's destiny demands nothing less. 6.

Judge Me By The

Footsteps I leave Behind

Author unknown

This is a story about a soldier who was finally coming home after having fought in Vietnam. Those of you who have seen my show in Branson or heard me speak on patriotism know how passionate I am about honoring our nation's servicemen and women. I can't remember who sent me this story but it moved me to tears. Your view of the Vietnam veteran is about change.

He called his parents from San Francisco. "Mom and Dad, I'm coming home, but I've got a favor to ask. I have a friend I'd like to bring with me." "Sure," they replied, "we'd love to meet him." "There's something you should know," the son continued. "He was hurt pretty badly in the fighting. He stepped on a land mine and lost an arm and a leg. He has nowhere else to go, and I want him to come live with us." "I'm sorry to hear that, son. Maybe we can help him find somewhere to live." "No, Mom and Dad, I want him to live with us." "Son," said the father, "you don't know what you're asking. Someone with such a handicap would be a terrible burden on us. We have our own lives to live, and we can't let something like this interfere with our lives. I think you should just come home and forget about this guy. He'll find a way to live on his own."

At that point, the son hung up the phone. The parents heard nothing more from him. A few days later, however, they received a call from the San Francisco police. They were told their son had died after falling from a building. The police believed it was suicide. The grief-stricken parents flew to San Francisco and were taken to the city morgue to identify the body of their son. They recognized him, but to their horror they also discovered something they didn't know, their son had only one arm and one leg.

The parents in this story are like many of us. We find it easy to love those who are good-looking or fun to have around, but we don't like people who inconvenience us or make us feel uncomfortable. We would rather stay away from people who aren't as healthy, beautiful, or smart as we are. Thankfully, there's someone who won't treat us that way. Someone who loves us with an unconditional love that welcomes us into the forever family, regardless of how messed up we are.

Tonight, before you tuck yourself in for the night, pray you will have the strength you need to accept people as they are, and to help us all be more understanding of those who are different from us as they could be someone in your family. 7.

My "Adopted" Brother

Many of you have met my "adopted" brother Tim Rogers.
There are so many things I admire about him it would take a
complete book for me to pen the praises. Given the opportunity
to describe Tim, these adjectives come to mind; Loyal, honorable,
passionate, dedicated, patriotic and "Christ-like." Now I know
I've raised a few eyebrows with that last description, but those of
you who've met Timmy you know what I mean. This is a man
who was not always a Believer... no way, in fact he was 180
degrees out of phase with "religion" not all that many years ago.
Let me tell you a little story about Tim and then you'll know why
I wanted to include "his story" in this book on patriotism.

Like millions of young Americans in the Vietnam era, Tim was
a rough and at times "cocky" G.I. who wanted to serve God,
Family and Country. As the war continued to escalate, Tim knew
his draft notice was expected to arrive any day. To make sure he
controlled his destiny, Tim decided to take control and enlist in
the United States Navy, the goal: Flight School. Tim's earliest
memory was dreaming about becoming an aviator, and the dream
was beginning to take wing. The first duty assignment found Tim
assigned to a S.A.R. (Search Air Rescue) outfit where he was
credited with saving many downed pilots who had ejected into
the ocean, or had their aircraft shot out from under them in the

jungles of Southeast Asia. While awaiting orders to report to flight school, he was called to rescue a downed pilot floating somewhere in the vastness of the oceans off Vietnam. The turning point came that day he rescued a downed Lt. Commander whose F-4 Phantom jet took a direct hit. As the story goes, this particular pilot was not doing too well in the choppy sea, he began to panic, threatening both himself and his rescuer. Tim, a 6'4" steely-eyed defender of American democracy realized there was only one way to calm the frantic aviator–abolish all sensory conscious mental activity. With a swift and powerful right hook, Tim transformed the stress-filled pilot into a unconscious subject with whom he could now work. Tim recalls thinking, "Oh, man what have I done? I just punched the lights out of the Lt. Commander! I knew my butt was gonna be in deep trouble." Following the successful retrieval, the chopper landed aboard the aircraft carrier. Shortly after the chopper blades stopped turning, Tim got word he was wanted in the debriefing room. And he knew he was in big trouble. But instead of being reprimanded, the Lt. Commander walked toward him holding out his right hand. The men vigorously shook hands, and while thanking Tim, he asked, "What is it you want to do in the Navy young man?" "Become a pilot sir." Tim replied. "Well then let's get you started on that mission." But God had other plans for Tim Rogers.

Before he could leave for basic flight school in Florida, one of the most incomprehensible accidents of war changed Tim's life forever. I won't go into the details of his injuries but he sustained such damage the medics actually put a toe-tag on his body that read; "Watch this one, he comes and goes." Tim "went" twelve times and "came back" thirteen! And it was a miracle because God had more for him to accomplish on this earth. Now, 32 years later, Tim Rogers is Branson's most loved veteran. Tony Orlando calls Tim his dearest friend. Being confined to a wheel-chair has it's challenges, but Tim has proven physical impairments can not hold back the spirit of God once its' flame begins inside a patriot's heart. Today, Tim is admired and respected for the man and patriot he has become. Now all these years later, he knows that God is using him to heal the hearts and minds of the thousands of Vietnam veterans who come to Branson. If you are lucky you will get to meet him, your heart will glow with pride as you realize Tim is more than a man sitting in a wheel-chair, he is truly a witness to his Lord's Glory and the healing power of the Holy Spirit. When you come to Branson, stop by Mike Radford's Remember When Veterans Cafe. It's inside The Radisson Hotel and dedicated to every veteran of all era's. Tim and I are always there before my Morning Shows, so hopefully you can come by and meet Tim, I promise, you'll be blessed.

Two Differing Chicago Legends

This is another of those anonymous stories sent to me over the great information highway. It gives great debate to whether it is our environment or heredity that leads to greatness. These stories certainly contradict each theory. No matter, I know you will enjoy.

Story number one:

World War II produced many heroes. One such man was Butch O'Hare. He was a fighter pilot assigned to an aircraft carrier in the South Pacific. One day his entire squadron was sent on a mission. After he was airborne, he looked at his fuel gauge and realized that someone had forgotten to top off his fuel tank. He would not have enough fuel to complete his mission and get back to his ship. His flight leader told him to return to the carrier. Reluctantly he dropped out of formation and headed back to the fleet. As he was returning to the mother-ship, he saw something that turned his blood cold, a squadron of Japanese Zeroes were speeding their way toward the American fleet.

The American fighters were gone on a sortie, a mission that left the fleet all but defenseless. He couldn't reach his squadron and bring them back in time to save the fleet. Nor, could he warn the fleet of the approaching danger. There was only one thing to do. He must somehow divert them from the fleet. Laying aside all thoughts of personal safety, he dove into the formation of Japanese planes. Wing-mounted 50 caliber's blazed as he charged in, attacking one surprised enemy plane and then another. Butch weaved in and out of the now broken formation and fired at as many planes as possible until finally all his ammunition was spent. Undaunted, he continued the assault. He dove at the Zeroes, trying to at least clip off a wing or tail, in hopes of damaging as many enemy planes as possible rendering them unfit to fly. He was desperate to do anything he could to keep them from reaching the American ships. Finally, the exasperated Japanese squadron took off in another direction. Deeply relieved, Butch O'Hare and his tattered fighter limped back to the carrier. Upon arrival he reported in and related the event surrounding his return. The film from the camera mounted on his plane told the tale. It showed the extent of Butch's daring attempt to protect his fleet. He was recognized as a hero and given one of the nation's highest military honors. And today, O'Hare Airport in Chicago is named in tribute to the courage of this great man. A real hero - a real Patriot.

Story number two:

In the gangster days a man lived in Chicago called Easy Eddie. At that time, Al Capone virtually owned the city. Capone wasn't famous for anything heroic. His exploits were anything but praiseworthy. He was, however, notorious for enmeshing the city of Chicago in everything from bootlegged booze and prostitution to murder. Easy Eddie was Capone's lawyer and for a good reason. He was very good! In fact, his skill at legal maneuvering kept Big Al out of jail for a long time. To show his appreciation, Capone paid him very well. Not only was the money big, Eddie got special dividends. For instance, he and his family occupied a fenced-in mansion with live-in help and all of the conveniences of the day. The estate was so large that it filled an entire Chicago city block. Yes, Eddie lived the high life of the Chicago mob and gave little consideration to the atrocity that went on around him. Eddie did have one soft spot, however. He had a son that he loved dearly. Eddy saw to it that his young son had the best of everything; clothes, cars, and a good education. Nothing was withheld. Price was no object. And, despite his involvement with organized crime, Eddie even tried to teach him right from wrong.

Yes, Eddie tried to teach his son to rise above his own sordid life. He wanted him to be a better man than he was. Yet, with all his wealth and influence, there were two things that Eddie couldn't give his son. Two things that Eddie sacrificed to the Capone mob that he could not pass on to his beloved son ... a good name and a good example. One day, Easy Eddie reached a difficult decision. Offering his son a good name was far more important than all the riches he could lavish on him. He had to rectify all the wrong that he had done. He would go to the authorities and tell the truth about Scar-face Al Capone. He would try to clean up his tarnished name and offer his son some semblance of integrity. To do this he must testify against the mob, and he knew that the cost would be great. But more than anything, he wanted to be an example to his son. He wanted to do his best to make restoration and hopefully have a good name to leave his son. So, he testified. Within the year, Easy Eddie's life ended in a blaze of gunfire on a lonely Chicago street. He had given his son the greatest gift he had to offer at the greatest price he would ever pay. I know what you're thinking. What do these two stories have to do with one another? Well, you see, Butch O'Hare was Easy Eddie's son. And as Paul Harvey says, "Now, you know the rest of the story." 8.

Be a legend to your children ... remember the power of example.

Meeting President Reagan

One of the things that I am most devoted to, is getting prayer back in schools. That one component in our children's school day would do so much to transform our nation back to the era when a child's innocence wasn't lost so early in life.

At our Remember When Theatre in Branson, I take an occasional, "pulse of America," because I want to know what's on people's minds. Believe me, people aren't shy when asked to share their opinions about the state of our nation. Before I get ahead of myself, you need to know I recently had a chat with a radio personality on a Springfield, Missouri "talk station." I asked him what he'd like me to talk about when he interviewed me on the show. "Your days in the Reagan White House!" he quickly added, "Tell me Mr. Reagan was as great as we all thought he was." And so began a dialogue about whom I consider not just a great communicator, but the man whose legacy created the great economy we all enjoy today. He was also the man most responsible for bringing an end to "The Evil Empire."

The year was 1981 and I had just accepted an appointment as a Special Advisor to The President's Council on Physical Fitness & Sports. The Chairman was the late George Allen. Everyone remembers him as the Head Coach of the Washington Redskins, a man who took "The Over-the-Hill-Gang" to the Superbowl in '72. Coach Allen was known as a man of amazing energy and doing things on a minutes notice. George called me one night about 9 o'clock in the evening and asked if I'd like to go to Washington to meet with the President. "You Bet!" I nearly shouted in the phone. Two hours later we boarded a DC 10 at LAX and took the "Red Eye" midnight flight to our nation's capitol.

Arriving at National Airport, now proudly known as Ronald Reagan National Airport, we were met by limo and whisked across town. Arriving at the guard gate the driver lowered his window. The White House guard recognized him, saluted smartly as the gates electronically swung open. Rounding the driveway we have seen a thousand times on TV we pulled under the pillars where another soldier stepped forward and opened the door. He immediately recognized George, then snapped to attention, "Welcome back Coach." I was in awe. It was hard to believe that I was walking inside The White House and in a few minutes would be sitting in a private meeting with our President. Mr. Reagan was the most charismatic and warm person I've ever met. He made me feel like we were old friends, "Hi Mike, he said. Just the fact he knew my name was overwhelming. I must make this very clear, the President knew me because I was a friend of his friend, Coach Allen. Nevertheless, just being in the same room with him was inspiring. There was an aura about him, a true magnatism that drew you in ... just about everyone who ever met him would tell you the same thing, he was magnetic and a true gentleman.

In the years since, I reminisce back to the last time I saw Mr. Reagan. The New York Mets had just won the World Series and Coach Allen and I stood as they presented the president with his official Mets jacket. It was one of those crisp fall days in Washington. The leaves had turned into a rainbow of color and the atmosphere around The White House was very cheerful. As the festivities in the rose garden ended, President Reagan thanked everyone for coming and walked down the sunlit hallway. Suddenly he turned and waved toward George and me. The famous smile and natural nod of his head acknowledged us in friendly recognition. That smile is what I most remember, his magnetic smile punctuated with his rosy cheeks. America will never see the likes of him again. He was truly an honored and respected gentleman. His respect for the Oval Office was so profound he would never remove his jacket. To do so, in his opinion, would dishonor the office he pledged to uphold.

This great land needs his kind again. America is in a moral crisis but its not too late to change our course. When I think of honorable Presidents, I see Ronald Reagan. I see General Dwight D. Eisenhower, FDR and Harry Truman. I see George Herbert Walker Bush. I see Jefferson, Washington and Abraham Lincoln. Men who believed in living their lives according to the Ten Commandments and The Bible, men who believed this is truly "One Nation Under God."

A Dad's Message to Congress

On Thursday, May 27, 1999, Darrell Scott, the father of Rachel Scott, a victim of the Columbine High School shootings in Littleton, Colorado was invited to address the House Judiciary Committee's sub-committee. What he said to our national leaders during this special session of Congress was painfully truthful. They were not prepared for what he was to say, nor was it received well. It needs to be heard by every parent, every politician, every sociologist, every psychologist, and every so-called expert. These courageous words spoken by Darrell Scott are powerful, penetrating, and deeply personal. There is no doubt that God sent this man as a voice crying in the wilderness. The following is a portion of the transcript of his comments:

"Since the dawn of creation there has been both good and evil in the hearts of men and women. We all contain the seeds of kindness or the seeds of violence. The death of my wonderful daughter, Rachel Joy Scott, and the death of that heroic teacher, and the other eleven children who died must not be in vain. Their blood cries out for answers." "The first recorded act of violence was when Cain slew his brother Abel out in the field. The villain was not the club he used. Neither was it the NCA, the National Club Association. The true killer was Cain, and the reason for the murder could only be found in Cain's heart.

"In the days that followed the Columbine tragedy, I was amazed at how quickly fingers began to be pointed at groups such as the NRA. I am not a member of the NRA. I am not a hunter. I do not even own a gun. I am not here to represent or defend the NRA because I don't believe that they are responsible for my daughter's death. Therefore I do not believe that they need to be defended. If I believed they had anything to do with Rachel's murder I would be their strongest opponent." "I am here today to declare that Columbine was not just a tragedy–it was a spiritual event that should be forcing us to look at where the real blame lies! Much of the blame lies here in this room. Much of the blame lies behind the pointing fingers of the accusers themselves."
"I wrote a poem just four nights ago that expresses my feelings best. This was written way before I knew I would be speaking here today:"

Your laws ignore our deepest needs, your words are empty air. You've stripped away our heritage, you've outlawed simple prayer. Now gunshots fill our classrooms, and precious children die. You seek for answers everywhere, and ask the question; "Why?"

You regulate restrictive laws, through legislative creed. And yet you fail to understand, that God is what we need!

"Men and women are three-part beings. We all consist of body, soul, and spirit. When we refuse to acknowledge a third part of our make-up, we create a void that allows evil, prejudice, and hatred to rush in and reek havoc. Spiritual influences were present within our educational systems for most of our nation's history. Many of our major colleges began as theological seminaries. This is a historical fact.

What has happened to us as a nation? We have refused to honor God, and in so doing, we open the doors to hatred and violence. And when something as terrible as Columbine's tragedy occurs—politicians immediately look for a scapegoat such as the NRA. They immediately seek to pass more restrictive laws that contribute to erode away our personal and private liberties. We do not need more restrictive laws. Eric and Dylan would not have been stopped by metal detectors. No amount of gun laws can stop someone who spends months planning this type of massacre. The real villain lies within our own political posturing and restrictive legislation are not the answers. The young people of our nation hold the key. There is a spiritual awakening taking place that will not be squelched! We do not need more religion. We do not need more gaudy television evangelists spewing out verbal religious garbage. We do not need more million dollar church buildings built while people with basic needs are being ignored. We do need a change of heart and a humble acknowledgment that this nation was founded on the principle of simple trust in God!"

"As my son Craig lay under that table in the school library and saw his two friends murdered before his very eyes–He did not hesitate to pray in school. I defy any law or politician to deny him that right! I challenge every young person in America, and around the world, to realize that on April 20, 1999, at Columbine High School prayer was brought back to our schools. Do not let the many prayers offered by those students be in vain. Dare to move into the new millennium with a sacred disregard for legislation that violates your God-given right to communicate with Him. To those of you who would point your finger at the NRA I give to you a sincere challenge. Dare to examine your own heart before casting the first stone! My daughter's death will not be in vain! The young people of this country will not allow that to happen!" 9.

Ask yourself this question: "What am I feeling right now?" When I first read this, my heart ached for the parents of these innocent martyrs. They were so young, filled with the expectations of fulfilling their "American Dreams." There are no words that will erase the heartbreak, there are no medications to heal the wounds in their hearts. Only lessons. But will people really learn? Did you really hear this father's words? The message I take from the Columbine tragedy is our nation is truly at great risk. When kids don't learn "Thou Shalt Not Kill"it leaves them open to the evil that sometimes creeps in and takes over the hearts of our young. Reread this story again and again until the obvious truths become part of your own thinking. Their deaths can and does have an impact on creating a rebirth of patriotism and the old-fashioned values that might have saved them.

Granny D's Day in Court

Most of us saw Doris "Granny D" Haddock as she marched across America in 1999. She was hiking to gain attention to her passionate belief in campaign finance reform. I sat and marveled at her energy, her spunk and it was obvious she was a patriot of the first order, a favorite of the nightly news. This was a great story; aging woman marching across our land to send a message to young and old alike. But what shocks me is the manner in which she was treated once she arrived in Washington D.C. You will be shaking your head when you learn what happened because she violated no law.

On Wednesday, May 24, 1999 in the District of Columbia court, "Granny D" plead guilty to the charge of demonstrating in the Capitol building on April 21st. Some 31 others were charged with her. This is a story I know you will pass along to all your friends who care about this land and who fear for the rights of even the weakest of our society. Try not to get as angry as I did, it's not good for your blood pressure.

Doris and the demonstrators were represented in court by attorney Mark Goldstone, who provided his services at a reduced rate. Doris and friends then picketed the $26 million dollar Democratic Party fundraiser at the Washington MCI Arena, where $500,000 fat cats sat at tables on the arena floor eating barbecue while listening to the President and Vice President. The "regular people," the $50 contributors had to pay $3 for a bottle of water to watch the others eat. Doris was well interviewed there by National Public Radio and several newspapers. When she crossed the street in front of the security-bristling arena, she was approached by a squad of six D.C. police. Soon thereafter she was arrested.

May 24, 2000 Court statement of Doris Haddock:

"Your Honor, the old woman who stands before you was arrested for reading the Declaration of Independence in America's Capitol Building. I did not raise my voice to do so and I blocked no hall. The First Amendment to the Constitution, Your Honor, says that Congress shall make no law abridging the freedom of speech, or of the press; or the right of the people peaceably to assemble and to petition the Government for a redress of grievances. So I cannot imagine what legitimate law I could have broken. We peaceably assembled there, Your Honor, careful to not offend the rights of any other citizen nor interrupt the peaceful enjoyment of their day. The people we met were supportive of what we were saying and I think they–especially the children–were shocked that we would be arrested for such a thoroughly wholesome American activity as respectfully voicing our opinion in our own hall. Any American standing there would have been shocked. For we were a most peaceable assembly, until the police came in with their bullhorns and their shackles to arrest us. One of us, who is here today, was injured and required a number of stitches to his head after he fell and could not break his own fall. He was detained for over four hours without medical care. I am glad we were only reading from the Declaration of Independence. I shudder to think what might have happened had we read from the Bill of Rights. I was reading from the Declaration of Independence to make the point that we must declare our independence from the corrupting bonds of big money in our election campaigns.

And so I was reading these very words when my hands were pulled behind me and bound: "We hold these truths to be self-evident, that all men are created equal, that they are endowed by their Creator with certain unalienable Rights, that among these are Life, Liberty and the pursuit of Happiness. That to secure these rights, Governments are instituted among Men, deriving their just powers from the consent of the governed, —That whenever any form of Government becomes destructive of these ends, it is the Right of the People to alter or to abolish it."

"Your Honor, we would never seek to abolish our dear United States. But alter it? Yes. it is our constant intention that it should be a government of, by and for the people, not the special interests, so that people may use this government in service to each other's needs and to protect the condition of our earth. Your Honor, it is now your turn to be a part of this arrest. If your concern is that we might have interfered with the visitor's right to a meaningful tour of their Capitol, I tell you that we helped them have a more meaningful one. If your concern is that we might have been blocking the halls of our government, let me assure you that we stood to one side of the Rotunda where we would not be in anyone's way. But I inform you that the halls are indeed blocked over there. They are blocked by the shameless sale of public policy to campaign contributors, which bars the doors and the halls to the people's legitimate needs and the flow of proper representation.

We Americans must put an end to it in any peaceful way that we can. Yes, we can speak when we vote, and we do. But we must also give our best effort to encourage the repair of a very broken system. We must do both."

"And the courts and prosecutors in government have a role, too. If Attorney General Reno would properly enforce the federal bribery statute, we would see lobbyists and elected officials dragged from the Capitol Building and the White House, their wrists tied, not ours. I would be home in New Hampshire, happily applauding the television news as my government cleaned its own house. In my 90 years, this is the first time I have been arrested. I risk my good name for I do indeed care what my neighbors think about me. But, Your Honor, some of us do not have much power, except to put our bodies in the way of an injustice to picket, to walk, or to just stand in the way. It will not change the world overnight, but it is all we can do. So I am here today while others block the halls with their corruption. Twenty-five million dollars are changing hands this very evening at a fund raiser down the street. It is the corrupt sale of public policy, and everyone knows it. I would refer those officials and those lobbyists, Your Honor, to Mr. Bob Dylan's advice when he wrote: "Come senators, congressmen, Please heed the call. Don't stand in the doorway, don't block up the hall."

"Your Honor, the song was a few years early, but the time has now come for change. The times are changing because they must. And they will sweep away the old politician the self-serving, the self-absorbed, the corrupt. The time of that leader is rapidly fading. We have come through a brief time when we have allowed ourselves to be entertained by corrupt and hapless leaders because they offer so little else, and because, as citizens, we have been priced out of participation and can only try to get some enjoyment out of their follies. But the earth itself can no longer afford them. We owe this change to our children and our grandchildren and our great grandchildren. We need have no fear that a self-governing people can creatively and effectively address their needs as a nation and a world if the corrupt and greedy are out of their way, and ethical leadership is given the helm."

"Your Honor, to the business at hand: the old woman who stands before you was arrested for reading the Declaration of Independence in America's Capitol Building. I did not raise my voice to do so and I blocked no hall. But if it is a crime to read the Declaration of Independence in our great hall, then I am guilty."

"Thank you very much."

The Judge, Chief Judge Hamilton of DC federal district court, was silent after Doris made her statement. In sentencing, he said to Doris and the demonstrators (this is an approximate statement until the court transcript becomes available): "Sometimes some people are ahead of the law. It will change, catching up to where they are. In the meantime, some people like you have to act on behalf of the silent masses." He went on for several minutes with a beautiful statement. He could have imposed sentences of six months imprisonment and $500. Instead, he reduced everyone's sentence to time already served, plus $10. He met with Doris in his chambers after the session and told her to "take care, because it is people like you who will help us reach our destiny." Some of his clerks were in tears at the conclusion of her heartfelt message and her display of passionate patriotism. 10.

Patriotic Ambassadors Avis Gutz and "The Commander" Arnold Dominguez

Shari and Mike with Presidential Candidate & U.S. Ambassador Alan Keyes.

SENATOR BOB DOLE
901 15TH STREET, N.W.
SUITE 410
WASHINGTON, D.C. 20005

August 16, 1999

Mr. Mike Radford
Remember When Theater
3562 Shepherd of the Hills Expressway
Branson, MO 65616

Dear Mike:

Thanks so much for your book. It really took me back to the days of fond memories and simpler times when God, family and country was the bedrock we all stood on. If your show is anything like your book, I am certain it is a winner as well.

I understand you give veterans, especially World War II veterans, a moving tribute during each of your shows. I commend you for doing this. We need to take every opportunity we can to say "Thank You" to all those who served and sacrificed so magnificently during World War II, as well as other conflicts. You are setting an outstanding example that all America needs to follow.

Thanks also for spearheading Branson's campaign to raise support for the National World War II Memorial. The efforts by the Branson community are sure to put your city on the map as a leading supporter of this long overdue tribute to America's greatest generation.

Again, thank you for everything and may God continue to bless you and your family.

Sincerely,

BOB DOLE

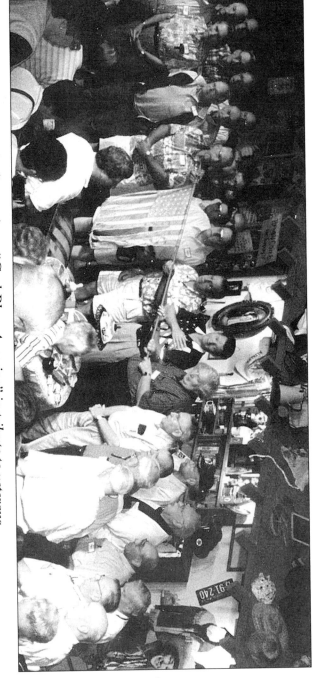

Audience sings, "God Bless America" in tribute to veterans

"Capt." Tim Rogers, Mike's "adopted" brother.

General Colin Powell and Mike discussing America's Promise.

Mike & Shari with "Best Pals" Sandy & Mike Ramirez (FBI-ret.)

MO State Rep. Sam Gaskill (veteran F-4 pilot), Mike, U.S. Congressman J.C. Watts

U. S. Department of Justice

Drug Enforcement Administration

Washington, D.C. 20537

April 23, 1993

Mike Radford
3516 Stein Blvd.
Eau Claire, WI   54701

Dear Mike,

Over the past seven years, your efforts have made a big impact on thousands of people who have heard your positive messages. Your gift is truly one of giving hope, encouragement, and direction.

It has been a pleasure working with you Mike, and you know if there is anything I can do to help, all you have to do is call.

Sincerely,

William F. Alden, Chief
Office of Congressional
and Public Affairs

PS: You were fantastic at our rally in New Orleans! The 10,000 people in the auditorium really enjoyed your presentation!

Fellow Patriot Glenn Witzenburg, a Branson's Veterans Memorial Museum partner.

In Wisconsin with Gov. Tommy Thompson.

Mike's "Hall of Heroes" Inside Radisson Hotel, Branson, MO

Mike joined Roy Rogers, Jr. on radio show.

Co-Hosting on PBS during WWII special.

*A true American hero, Gen. Paul Tibbets, pilot of the Enola Gay
which dropped the bomb ending WWII.*

THE PRESIDENT'S COUNCIL ON PHYSICAL FITNESS AND SPORTS
WASHINGTON, D.C. 20001

September 14, 1988

Michael J. Radford
Special Advisor
National Fitness Foundation
2250 E. Imperial Highway Suite 412
El Segundo, CA 90245

Dear Michael,

President Reagan asked me to pass along his gratitude for all your hard work.

When I asked you to address The Republican Governor's Conference in White Plains, I knew you would do a great job and be a tremendous addition to the program. Once again my coaching instincts didn't let me down. Your talk on mentoring is years ahead of its time and I know the Governor's were very impressed with your ideas. Keep up the good work.

Again, thank you for all you are doing to motivate Americans to reach new levels of achievement and happiness. I am proud to have you on my team.

Your Friend Always,

George

George H. Allen
Chairman
President's Council on Physical Fitness & Sports

GHA/bt

Dennis K. Showers, Mike's best friend killed in Vietnam.

Mickey Showers, Denny's mom, a former "Rosie" in WWII.

Don & Helen Griffith "Mommie Helen," Mike & Shari.

*Mike hugs Denny Shower's mother during veteran tribute.
Denny's Dad, Frank, to her left.*

Mrs. Missouri, Tara Sukman, Jimmie Rodgers, Sen. John Ashcroft, Shari & Mike.

Branson's "Rat-Pack." Front: Shari, Tim Rogers, Gayle Kirchner.
Back row: Mike, Beverly Dillard & Rodney Dillard, Tony & Francine Orlando.

*WWII veteran Tim LaHaye, co-Author of
"Left Behind" Books.*

Mike's Theatre manager, MSgt. Tony & Judy Gallagher.

Fellow patriot Tony Orlando

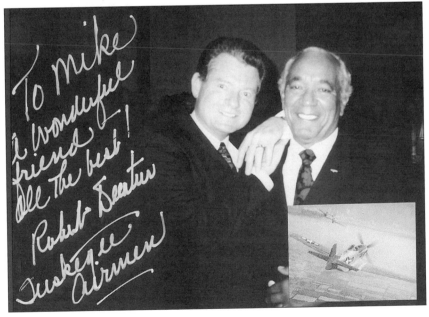

With Judge Robert Decatur, "Tuskegee Airman."

*"Official" ribbon cutting, Mike's Veterans Cafe, Radisson Hotel.
Senator John Ashcroft cuts ribbon, Branson mayor Lou Schaefer to his left.*

Veterans are always honored during every show, or speech Mike gives.

Mary & Bob Smiley; Mike, JoAnne & Walt Pulkinen at Smiley Group Conference, Scottsdale, AZ

The Smiley Group "Patriots" during Scottsdale Business Conference. Singing "God Bless America."

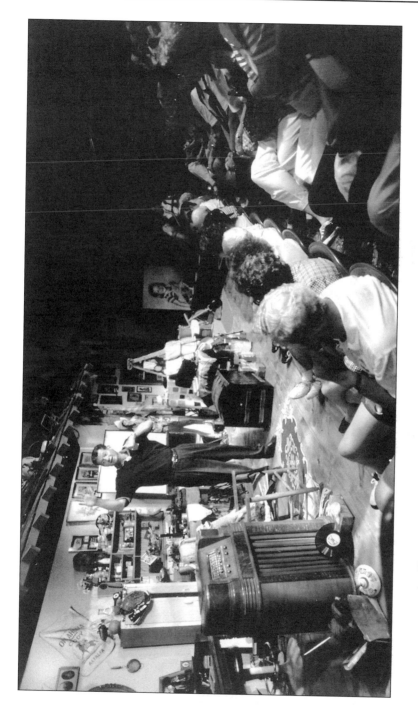

Audiences sit "up close & personal" at Mike's Remember When Theatre.

PHOTO BY: Plumlee Photography, Oak Grove, AR

An evening with General Colin Powell at the College of the Ozarks

Dinner at The Radfords, Tony Orlando and Jimmie "Honeycomb" Rodgers.

The Jacobson's of Branson give historical map to Mike's "Hall of Heroes" display.

With Army Col. Ben Purcell, 5½ years in "Hanoi Hilton."

An evening with Gen. H. Norman Schwartzkopf.

During his show, Mike had a young patriot on stage.

The Smiley Family TeachingPatriotism:
l to r: Mariah, Kelli, Garrett & Scott

102-year-young Charles Buckner, WWI & WWII veteran.

A Canadian's View of America

I wear a Roy Rogers wrist-watch. I do it because I know each time I look to see the time, I see my hero standing next to his wife Dale. Silly? Nostalgic? Cute? The reason I wear a Roy Rogers wrist watch is each time I glance at it, I am reminded of the kind of man I strive to be. A loyal husband. A good role model. A passionate Patriot. All descriptions of the man who influenced millions of us "Boomers." There is another man I came to admire recently. I never met him. Probably never heard his broadcasts because he worked for over forty years in Canada. His name was Gordon Sinclair. Mr. Sinclair was a man known to "Tell it like it is." And I admire that. I try to be truthful in all my daily endeavors and those who know me say I indeed speak my mind. I'm sorry I never got to meet Gordon Sinclair because I know I would have liked him. He was a colorful figure in 20th Century journalism. For nearly five decades he produced a daily radio series called "Let's Be Personal;" he gained a reputation for honesty and became popular to millions of listeners. Sinclair is especially remembered for a broadcast he made praising the United States on June 5, 1973. The text of that broadcast, known as, "The Americans," is widely circulated on the internet and I will include it here because he understood much of what many American's don't. Here is the text of his views on our beloved country:

On June 5, 1973, Gordon Sinclair sat up in bed in Toronto and turned on his TV set. The United States had just pulled out of the Vietnam war which had ended in a stalemate - a war fought daily on TV, over the radio and in the press. The aftermath of that war resulted in a world-wide sell-off of American investments, prices tumbled, the United States economy was in trouble. The war had also divided the American people, at home and abroad it seemed everyone was lambasting the United States.

He turned on his radio, twisted the dial and turned it off. He picked up the morning paper. In print, he saw in headlines what he had found on TV and radio - the Americans were taking a verbal beating from nations around the world. Disgusted with what he saw and heard, he was outraged!

At 10:30, he walked into his office and "dashed-off" two pages in 20 minutes for LET'S BE PERSONAL for the 11:45 am broadcast. He then turned to writing his 11:50 newscast that was to follow. At 12:01 pm, the script for LET'S BE PERSONAL was dropped on the desk of his secretary who scanned the pages for a suitable heading and then wrote "Americans" across the top and filed it away. The phones were already ringing.

"LET'S BE PERSONAL"
Broadcast June 5, 1973 CFRB, Toronto, Ontario

Topic: "The Americans"

"The United States dollar took another pounding on German, French and British exchanges this morning, hitting the lowest point ever known in West Germany. It has declined there by 41% since 1971 and this Canadian thinks it is time to speak up for the Americans as the most generous and possibly the least-appreciated people in all the earth.

As long as sixty years ago, when I first started to read newspapers, I read of floods on the Yellow River and the Yangtse. Who rushed in with men and money to help? The Americans did.

They have helped control floods on the Nile, the Amazon, the Ganges and the Niger. Today, the rich bottom-land of the Mississippi is under water and no foreign land has sent a dollar to help. Germany, Japan and, to a lesser extent, Britain and Italy, were lifted out of the debris of war by the Americans who poured in billions of dollars and forgave other billions in debts. None of those countries is today paying even the interest on its remaining debts to the United States.

When the franc was in danger of collapsing in 1956, it was the Americans who propped it up and their reward was to be insulted and swindled on the streets of Paris. I was there. I saw it.

When distant cities are hit by earthquakes, it is the United States that hurries in to help... Managua Nicaragua is one of the most recent examples. So far this spring, 59 American communities have been flattened by tornadoes. Nobody has helped.

110

The Marshall Plan – the Truman Policy, ... all pumped billions upon billions of dollars into discouraged countries. Now, newspapers in those countries are writing about the decadent war-mongering Americans. I'd like to see one of those countries that is gloating over the erosion of the United States dollar build its own airplanes.

Come on... let's hear it! Does any other country in the world have a plane to equal the Boeing Jumbo Jet, the Lockheed Tristar or the Douglas DC 10? If so, why don't they fly them? Why do all international lines except Russia fly American planes? Why does no other land on earth even consider putting a man or women on the moon?

You talk about Japanese technocracy and you get radios. You talk about German technocracy and you get automobiles. You talk about American technocracy and you find men on the moon, not once, but several times ... and safely home again. You talk about scandals and the Americans put theirs right in the store window for everyone to look at.

Even the draft dodgers are not pursued and hounded. They are here on our streets, most of them ... unless they are breaking Canadian laws ... are getting American dollars from Ma and Pa at home to spend here.

When the Americans get out of this bind ... as they will... who could blame them if they said 'the hell with the rest of the world'. Let someone else buy the Israel bonds, Let someone else build or

111

repair foreign dams or design foreign buildings that won't shake apart in earthquakes.

When the railways of France, Germany and India were breaking down through age, it was the Americans who rebuilt them. When the Pennsylvania Railroad and the New York Central went broke, nobody loaned them an old caboose. Both are still broke. I can name to you 5,000 times when the Americans raced to the help of other people in trouble.

Can you name me even one time when someone else raced to the Americans in trouble? I don't think there was outside help even during the San Francisco earthquake.

Our neighbors have faced it alone and I am one Canadian who is damned tired of hearing them kicked around. They will come out of this thing with their flag high. And when they do, they are entitled to thumb their nose at the lands that are gloating over their present troubles.

I hope Canada is not one of these. But there are many smug, self-righteous Canadians. And finally, the American Red Cross was told at its 48th Annual meeting in New Orleans this morning that it was broke.

This year's disasters, with the year less than half-over...has taken it all and nobody...but nobody... has helped."

ORIGINAL SCRIPT COURTESY STANDARD BROAD-CASTING CORPORATION LTD. © 1973 BY GORDON SINCLAIR PUBLISHED BY STAR QUALITY MUSIC

(SOCAN) A DIVISION OF UNIDISC MUSIC INC. 578
HYMUS BOULEVARD — POINTE-CLAIRE, QUEBEC,
CANADA, H9R 4T2

Gordon Sinclair could not have written a book that could have
had a greater impact in the world than his two-page script for
THE AMERICANS. A book should have been written on the
events that followed. But, no one, including Sinclair himself,
could have envisioned the reaction of the people of the United
States - from presidents - state governors - Congress - the Senate
- all media including TV, radio, newspapers, magazines - and from
the "ordinary" American on the street. Nor, could have the
Canadian government - stunned by the response to what has
come to be regarded as one of Canada's greatest public relations
feats in the history of our relations with the United States of
America.

But, how did Sinclair's tribute to Americans reach them? It had
been swept across the United States at the speed of a prairie fire
by American radio stations - first, a station in Buffalo called and
asked to be fed a tape copy of the broadcast with permission to
use - both freely given. Nearby American stations obtained
copies from Buffalo or called direct. By the time it reached the
Washington, DC area, a station had superimposed Sinc's broadcast over an instrumental version of BRIDGE OVER TROU-
BLED WATER, and was repeating it at fixed times several times
a day.

Congressmen and Senators heard it. It was read several times into the Congressional Record. A recording contract was signed. As they were finalizing a contract that would see all royalties which would normally be due Gordon Sinclair be paid (at his request) to the American Red Cross. Word was received that an unauthorized record, using Sinclair's script but read by another broadcaster, was already flooding the US market. (Subsequently, on learning that this broadcaster had agreed to turn over his royalties to the Red Cross, no legal action was taken).

Sinclair's recording of his own work (to which Avco had added a stirring rendition of THE BATTLE HYMN OF THE REPUBLIC) did finally reach record stores, and sold hundreds of thousands of copies, but the potential numbers were depressed by the sale of the infringing record. Other record producers and performers (including Tex Ritter) obtained legal permission to make their own versions. In Ritter's case, because of the first-person style of the script, Tex preceded his performance with a proper credit to Sinclair as the author. The American Red Cross received millions of dollars in royalties, and Gordon Sinclair was present at a special ceremony acknowledging his donation.

Advertisers using print media contacted CFRB for permission to publish the text in a non-commercial manner; industrial plants asked for the right to print the script in leaflet form to handout to their employees.

Gordon Sinclair received invitations to attend and be honored at many functions in the United States which, by number and due to family health problems at the time, he had to decline. However, CFRB newscaster Charles Doering, was flown to Washington to give a public reading of THE AMERICANS to the 28th National Convention of the United States Air Force Association, held September 18, 1974 at the Sheraton Park Hotel. His presentation was performed with the on-stage backing of the U.S. Air Force Concert Band, joined by the 100-voice Singing Sergeants in a special arrangement of The Battle Hymn of the Republic.

Eight years after the first broadcast of THE AMERICANS, U.S. President Ronald Reagan made his first official visit to Canada. At the welcoming ceremonies on Parliament Hill, the new President praised, "the Canadian journalist who wrote that (tribute)" to the United States when it needed a friend. Prime Minister Pierre Trudeau had Sinclair flown to Ottawa to be his guest at the reception that evening.

Sinc had a long and pleasant conversation with Mr. Reagan. The President told him that he had a copy of the record of THE AMERICANS at his California ranch home when he was governor of the state, and played it from time to time when things looked gloomy.

On the evening of May 15th, 1984, following a regular day's broadcasting, Gordon Sinclair suffered a heart attack. He died on May 17th. As the word of his illness spread throughout the

United States, calls inquiring about his condition had been received from as far away as Texas. The editorial in the Sarasota Herald-Tribune of May 28th was typical of the reaction of the United States news media - A GOOD FRIEND PASSES ON.

U.S. President Ronald Reagan: "I know I speak for all Americans in saying the radio editorial Gordon wrote in 1973 praising the accomplishments of the United States was a wonderful inspiration. It was not only critics abroad who forgot this nation's many great achievements, but even critics here at home. Gordon Sinclair reminded us to take pride in our nation's fundamental values."

Former Prime Minister Pierre Trudeau: "Gordon Sinclair's death ends one of the longest and most remarkable careers in Canadian Journalism. His wit, irreverence, bluntness and off-beat views have been part of the media landscape for so long that many Canadians had come to believe he would always be there."

Following a private family service, two thousand people from all walks of life filled Nathan Phillips Square in front of Toronto's City Hall for a public service of remembrance organized by Mayor Art Eggleton. Dignitaries joining him on the platform were Ontario Lieutenant Governor, John Black Aird; the Premier of Ontario, William Davis; and Metro Chairman Paul Godfrey. Tens of thousands more joined them through CFRB's live broadcast of the service which began symbolically at 11:45 - the regular time of Sinc's daily broadcast of LET'S BE

PERSONAL. As Ontario Premier William Davis said of him, "The name could become the classic definition of a full life." 11.

Tie A Yellow Ribbon

Mention the title and people automatically think of Tony Orlando's hit song. Why? Because it epitomizes the word "freedom." When Tony recorded the hit back in the 70s, nobody expected it to become mega hit let alone an icon. But it did both, big time.

In a very dramatic event, Orlando was asked to sing his famous song to all the returning POWs from Vietnam. As 25,000 cheered, Tony sang to the returning heroes, as tears flowed freely.

Today Tony and his lovely wife Francine live in Branson atop a beautiful hillside overlooking Tablerock Lake. The house is just what you might expect from a super star, large, filled with expensive furnishings and walls covered with Gold Records and memorabilia from over forty years in show business. But there is something else inside the Orlando home: unqualified love and respect.

I first met Tony nearly seven years ago when we first opened our show in Branson. His operations manager, Bob Honn had befriended Shari and me a few days earlier when I stopped to admire his new Chevy Blazer. Bob Honn is just one of those guys you like the moment you meet him. My manager in New York, Ben Carrizzo had worked with Tony in the past, so naturally we all wanted to see Tony's show at his new "Yellow Ribbon Theatre." We weren't disappointed. The nearly 2000 people in the audience was treated to a show that pulled out all the stops.

Countless standing ovations and cheers so loud it made your ears ring. It was wonderful. And now years later Tony and Frannie continue to amaze us with their friendship, it's a bond we cherish.

Tony Orlando is a gentle man and a passionate patriot. There are countless stories that I could tell about his patriotism but Tony chooses to do his "thing" quietly and without fanfare. He believes, as I do, our veterans are the true heroes of our society, and Tony will continue to dedicate his life to honoring these honorable men and women of service.

We Need More Reporters Like Nick!

There aren't many news reporters who are willing to go against whatever is a current popular "cause" - and be castigated for being insensitive. We tip our hats to Mr. Gholson. And a special thanks to the Times Record News for allowing me to share this story with you. When I called the newsroom recently, a friendly reporter named Bruce Smith took my call, "Just make sure you give the paper and Nick a good plug in your book." I promised I would, so here it is and now, on with the story.

From the TIMES RECORD NEWS, Wichita Falls, Texas:

So Sue Me!

By: NICK GHOLSON:

Some people, it seems, get offended way too easily. I mean, isn't that what all this prayer hullabaloo is all about - people getting offended? Those of us in the majority are always tippy-toeing around, trying to make sure we don't step on the toes or hurt the feelings of the humorless. And you can bet there's a lawyer standing on every corner making sure we don't. Take this prayer deal. It's absolutely ridiculous. Some atheist goes to a high school football game, hears a kid say a short prayer before the game and gets offended. So he hires a lawyer and goes to court and asks somebody to pay him a whole bunch of money for all the damage done to him. You would have thought the kid kicked him in the crotch. Damaged for life by a 30-second prayer?

Am I missing something here? I don't believe in Santa Claus, but I'm not going to sue somebody for singing a Ho-Ho-Ho song in December. I don't agree with Darwin, but I didn't go out and hire a lawyer when my high school teacher taught his theory of evolution. Life, liberty or your pursuit of happiness will not be endangered because someone says a 30-second prayer before a football game. So what's the big deal? It's not like somebody is up there reading the entire book of Acts. They're just talking to a God they believe in and asking him to grant safety to the players on the field and the fans going home from the game. "But it's a Christian prayer," some will argue. Yes, and this is the United States of America, a country founded on Christian principles. And we are in the Bible belt. According to our very own phone book, Christian churches outnumber all others better than 200-to-1. So what would you expect - somebody chanting Hare Krishna? If I went to a football game in Jerusalem, I would expect to hear a Jewish prayer. If I went to a soccer game in Baghdad, I would expect to hear a Muslim prayer. If I went to a ping pong match in China, I would expect to hear someone pray to Buddha. And I wouldn't be offended. It wouldn't bother me one bit. When in Rome...

"But what about the atheists?" is another argument. What about them? Nobody is asking them to be baptized. We're not going to pass the collection plate. Just humor us for 30 seconds. If that's asking too much, bring a Walkman or a pair of ear plugs. Go to the bathroom. Visit the concession stand. Call your lawyer. Unfortunately, one or two will make that call. One or two will tell thousands what they can and cannot do. I don't think a short prayer at a football game is going to shake the world's foundations. Nor do I believe that not praying will result in more serious injuries on the field or more fatal car crashes after the game. In fact, I'm not so sure God would even be at all these games if he didn't have to be. Christians are just sick and tired of turning the other cheek while our courts strip us of all our rights. Our parents and grandparents taught us to pray before eating, to pray before we go to sleep. Our Bible tells us just to pray without ceasing. Now a handful of people and their lawyers are telling us to cease praying. God, help us. And if that last sentence offends you–well, just sue me. [12.]

The Great State of Kansas

Senator Bob Dole is a gentleman from Kansas that attained all but the highest office in our land. But did you ever consider what influenced him most and what circumstances propelled him to the heights of political success? How he became the statesman, the presidential candidate is the stuff of a true legend. How he did it is, in my opinion a combination of influences. His belief in God, his family who stood behind him when he left for W.W. II and stood beside him when he returned with near fatal battle injuries. Another part of his make-up was carved by the values his country was known for: Duty, Honor, Service.

What is it about Kansas and it's citizenry that seems to always stand firm for old-fashioned patriotism? I think the following story helps to answer the question.

When Minister Joe Wright was asked to open the new session of the Kansas Senate in 1999, everyone was expecting the same style, the usual politically-correct generalities, but what they heard was a stirring prayer delivered with passion calling our country to repentance and righteousness. The response was instantaneous. A number of legislators walked out during the prayer in protest. In six short weeks, the Central Christian Church had logged more than 5,000 phone calls with only 47 of those calls responding negatively. The church is now receiving international requests for copies of the prayer from every point on the globe. In fact Paul Harvey aired the prayer and "The Rest of the Story" on his radio broadcasts, receiving the largest response than any other story he has reported.

The Prayer:

Heavenly Father, we come before you today to ask Your forgiveness and see Your direction and guidance. We know Your Word says, "Woe on those who call evil good," but that's exactly what we have done. We have lost our spiritual equilibrium and reversed our values. We confess that:

We have ridiculed the absolute truth of Your Word and called it pluralism.

We have worshiped other gods and called it
multi-culturalism.

We have endorsed perversion and called it an
alternative lifestyle.

We have exploited the poor and called it the lottery.

We have neglected the needy and called it welfare.

We have rewarded laziness and called it welfare.

We have killed our unborn children and called it a choice.

We have shot abortionists and called it justifiable.

We have neglected to discipline our children
and called it building self-esteem.

We have abused power and called it political savvy.

We have coveted our neighbor's possessions and
called it ambition.

We have polluted the air with profanity and
pornography and called it freedom of expression.

We have ridiculed the time-honored values of our
forefathers and called it enlightenment.
Search us, O God, and know our hearts today;
cleanse us from every sin and set us free.

Guide and Bless these men and women who have
been sent to direct us to the center of Your will.
I ask it in the name of your Son,
the living Savior, Jesus Christ. Amen. [13.]

Kansas has much to be proud. Thank you Minister Joe Wright
for setting an example for us to follow. As many of you know,
Col. Bob Patrick and Senator Dole asked me to spearhead the
fundraising efforts in Branson to help build The W.W.II
Memorial in Washington, D.C. I was honored to be a part of the
team responsible in paying tribute to, "The Greatest
Generation." It isn't an accident that one of Kansas' most loved
sons led the effort. The long overdue memorial will stand for
centuries in honor of all who served and died for our liberty.
We owe so much to so many.

I Pledge Allegiance...

When I was a little kid growing up in northern California, I remember vividly how proud we all felt each and every morning when our teacher would ask us to stand up and say the pledge of allegiance. It wasn't a task we dreaded or moaned about... we were happy to do it. The day wouldn't have started right if we didn't place our hands over our hearts and say those words that meant so much. It unified the classroom. It justified who we were and what our lives were all about. Maybe that explains why many kids today don't seem to know who they are, or what they stand for. Back in the 30s, 40s and 50s we all knew what we were, we were Americans and darned proud of it too!

In the final minutes during my Branson show, I bring out my Grandma Harriet's old forty-eight star flag. The fabric is very old and deteriorating rapidly. I explain to the audience that Grandma's flag clearly represents the state of affairs in America today. Our founding fathers selected blue to represent "loyalty"— the faded color shows how loyalty has deteriorated in our society. The red stripes were sewn into "old glory" to honor the blood of our patriots. The white stripes represent "purity" in our society. In my Grandma's old flag, the white stripes are torn and ragged. Which, to me at least, demonstrates how the moral fabric of our nation is also tattered and torn. We as a country are in the depths of a moral crisis. When you look at the red stripes on my

Grandma's flag, you will see not one is tattered or torn, proving none of our family's sacrifices, or any of our patriots blood was shed in vein, because this still is "One Nation Under God."

Here is a poem sent to me that should be framed and hung on the wall for every child in America. This appeared in Dear Abby's column in 1999.

"Remember Me?"

By, David C. Graham

"Hello... Remember me? Some people call me Old Glory, others call me The Star Spangled Banner, but whatever they call me, I am your flag, the flag of the United States of America.

Something has been bothering me, so I thought I might talk it over with you–because it is about you and me. I remember some time ago, people would line up on both sides of the street to watch the parade, and naturally I was leading every one, proudly waving in the breeze.

When your daddy saw me coming, he immediately removed his hat and placed it against this left shoulder so that his hand was directly over his heart—remember? And you, I remember were standing there, straight as a soldier. You didn't have a hat, but you were giving the right salute. Remember your little sister? Not to be outdone, she was saluting the same as you with her right hand over her heart—remember?

What happened? I'm still the same old flag. Oh, I've added a few more stars since those parades of long ago. But now, somehow, I don't feel as proud as I used to feel. When I come down your street, you just stand there with your hands in your pockets. You may give me a small glance, and then you look away. I see children running around you shouting; they don't seem to know who I am.

I saw one man take his hat off, then he looked around and when he didn't see anybody else take off their hat, he quickly put his on again. Is it a sin to be patriotic today? Have you forgotten what I stand for, and where I have been? Anzio, Guadalcanal, Iwo Jima, Korea, Vietnam, and Desert Storm!

Take a look at the memorial honor rolls, and see the names of those patriotic Americans who gave their lives to keep this republic free. When you salute me, you are actually saluting THEM. Well, it won't be long until I'll be coming down your street again. So when you see me, please stand straight and place your hand over your heart and I'll know that you remembered... and then I'll salute YOU... by waving back." [14].

During the veterans' salute in my Branson show, I read Mr. Graham's words to hopefully spark an interest in this "thing" called patriotism. Too many young people don't have a clue why us "older" people are so passionate about the subject. What they don't know could literally kill them. For when our freedoms are taken away, the indomitable human spirit will revolt in protest. Its imperative we all stand up for our sovereignty so those who want to eliminate it, will know, just as the British learned, "Don't Tread on Me!"

One man I greatly admire is a Vietnam veteran named Sam Gaskill. Sam serves in the Missouri House of Representatives and stands proudly for his God, Family and Country. We were talking one day about the state of patriotism in America and he told me about a bill he proposed in the Missouri house. Mr. Gaskill's bill says that yes, people have the right to protest and burn the flag as a form of their first amendment right to free speech. His bill says, and I paraphrase, "If I, or any other citizen who loves the Star-Spangled Banner catches you doing it ... we have the right to beat the crap out of you without the threat of legal action against us!" Thank you Representative Gaskill for having the courage to stand up for what is right. I encourage all of you to do the same because millions of boys and girls died fighting for that flag. Let's honor their memory by protecting it from the idiots who have far too much time on their hands and have no concept of defending the memory of our fallen heroes.

One Nation Under God

Here's another fascinating tid-bit about our currency that I received over the internet. Again it's author is anonymous. I know you'll be amazed—

"Take out a one dollar bill and look at it. The one dollar bill you're looking at first came off the presses in 1957 in its present design. This so-called paper money is in fact a cotton and linen blend, with red and blue minute silk fibers running through it. It is actually material. We've all washed it without it falling apart. A special blend of ink is used, the contents we will never know. It is overprinted with symbols and then it is starched to make it water resistant and pressed to give it that nice crisp look.

If you look on the front of the bill, you will see the United States Treasury Seal. On the top you will see the scales for the balance - a balanced budget. In the center you have a carpenter's T-square, a tool used for an even cut. Underneath is the Key to the United States Treasury. That's all pretty easy to figure out, but what is on the back of that dollar bill is something we should all know. If you turn the bill over, you will see two circles. Both circles, together, comprise the Great Seal of the United States. The First Continental Congress requested that Benjamin Franklin and a group of men come up with a Seal. It took them four years to accomplish this task and another two years to get it approved. If you look at the left hand circle, you will see a Pyramid. Notice the face is lighted and the western side is dark. This country was just beginning. We had not begun to explore the West or decided what we could do for Western Civilization. The Pyramid is uncapped, again signifying that we were not even close to being finished. Inside the capstone you have the all-seeing eye, an ancient symbol for divinity. It was Franklin's belief that one man couldn't do it alone, but a group of men, with the help of God, could do anything. "IN GOD WE TRUST" is on this currency. The Latin above the pyramid, ANNUIT COEPTIS, means "God has favored our undertaking." The Latin below the pyramid, NOVUS ORDO SECLORUM, means "a new order has begun." At the base of the pyramid is the Roman Numeral for 1776. If you look at the right-hand circle, and check it carefully, you will learn that it is on every National Cemetery in the United States. It is also on the Parade of Flags Walkway at the Bushnell, Florida National Cemetery and is the centerpiece of most hero's monuments. Slightly modified, it is the seal of the President of the United States and it is always visible whenever he speaks, yet no one knows what the symbols mean. The Bald Eagle was selected as a symbol for victory for two reasons: first, he is not afraid of a storm; he is strong and he is smart enough to soar above it. Secondly, he wears no material crown. We had just broken from the King of England. Also, notice the shield is unsupported. This country can now stand on it's own. At the top of that shield you have a white bar signifying congress, a unifying factor. We were coming together as one nation. In the Eagle's beak you will read, "E PLURIBUS UNUM", meaning "one nation from many people." Above the Eagle you have thirteen stars representing the thirteen original colonies, and any clouds of misunderstanding rolling away. Again, we were coming together as one. Notice what the Eagle holds in his talons. He holds an olive branch and arrows. This country wants peace, but we will never be afraid to fight to preserve peace. The Eagle always wants to face the olive branch, but in time of war, his gaze turns toward the arrows. They say that the number 13 is an unlucky number. This is almost a worldwide belief. You will usually never see a room numbered 13, or any hotels or motels with a 13th floor. But think about this: 13 original colonies, 13 signers of the Declaration of Independence, 13 stripes on our flag, 13 steps on the Pyramid, 13 letters in the Latin above, 13 letters in "E Pluribus Unum", 13 stars above the Eagle, 13 plumes of feathers on each span of the Eagle's wing, 13 bars on that shield, 13 leaves on the olive branch, 13 fruits, and if you look closely, 13 arrows. And for minorities: the 13th Amendment. I always ask people, "Why don't you know this?" Your children don't know this and their history teachers don't know it either. Too many patriots have sacrificed too much to ever let the symbolic meaning fade. Many veterans remember coming home to an America that didn't care. Too many never came home at all. We need to tell everyone what's on the back of the one dollar bill and what it stands for, because nobody else will if we don't. 15.

There is one thing I would like to see happen in our schools but it will take a great many patriotic Americans to demand it's emplacement. We Bible believers must lead the way in returning to every classroom in The United States of America the follow-ing:

The Ten Commandments

1. Thou shalt have no other gods before me.

2. Thou shalt not take the name of the Lord thy God in vain

3. Thou shalt not make unto thee any graven image.

4. Remember the sabbath day, to keep it Holy.

5. Honor thy father and thy mother.

6. Thou shalt not kill.

7. Thou shalt not commit adultery.

8. Thou shall not steal.

9. Thou shalt not bear false witness against thy neighbor.

10. Thou shalt not covet thy neighbor's house, thou shalt not covet thy neighbor's wife, nor any thing that is thy neighbor's.

There are many in our land who think these "radical" old-fashioned concepts have no place in our public schools. I have but one question for these folks, "How well has our society fared since Ms. O'Hare got God kicked out of school?" The answer is obvious. The moral free-fall and decline in decency has escalated to near light-speed. As long as there are tests given in school, there will be prayer! Nobody can stop it. Now it's time to look back, to rekindle the flames that our nation was founded upon. When our leaders were all men of God and looked to our heavenly Father for wisdom and guidance. Even George Washington was looked upon as a man whose destiny was shaped by the very hand of God Almighty. Think about this, would you rather continue down the path we have witnessed or return to the days when American children were free to stand together and recite these wonderful words:

"I pledge allegiance to the flag of the United States of America. And to the republic for which it stands, one nation under God, indivisible, with liberty and justice for all."

One of my new heroes is a man named David Barton. He founded WallBuilders, Incorporated, a Bible believing business whose mission is paralleled in the title of this book. My "adopted" brother told me about David's work and suggested I read some of his work. One story above all others grabbed me. Its the true story of a young George Washington, a Colonel, only 23 years-old and the battle that was to become legend. The sad part is this account of God's protective shield was never taught in our schools. The battle on the Monongahela (PA) was certainly one of the most significant events of his early life. A life that literally was shielded by unseen Angels of protection. Approximately fifteen years after the battle, the Chief of the Indian Tribe Washington had fought requested a private audience with the military man he, the Chieftain was assigned to kill in the battle years earlier. I will paraphrase, in first person, the Chieftains account of what took place:

He began to speak telling Washington that he was the Chief and ruled over his tribes. His influence extending from the Great Lakes to the far mountains. He told of traveling a very long way just to meet the young warrior of the great battle so long ago. The Chief told of shouting to his braves who were marksmen of the first order to make sure their aim was perfect and true to their target, the young Col. Washington. As instructed the Indian warriors leveled their guns and took perfect aim at the horseman now riding only feet away. The triggers were pulled, sparks igniting gun-powder propelling lead balls which each violently found their mark, ripping through Washington's coat. One Indian warrior hit his target with perfection, not once but several times but the rider stayed mounted. Another marksman pulled his trigger, again the bullet ripped through Washington's coat but still he rode. A third hit his mark, then a fourth and fifth but the rider remained upright and strong. Seeing his marksmen had indeed aimed true and deadly, the Chieftain vowed one day to pay homage to this white warrior who was protected by God. The Chieftain recalled, "Our rifles were leveled, rifles which, but for you, knew not how to miss but it was all in vain for a power mightier than we shielded you. I have come to pay homage to the man who was protected from Heaven, and who can never die in battle." 16.

When I first heard of "The Bullet Proof Washington," I thought the Indians had missed their mark. But in recounting the incident years later, a President Washington verified the facts telling astonished listeners that he indeed had several bullet holes that penetrated the chest of his coat, but not a bruise could be found. What is amazing is that both the Indian warriors and their intended victim told the same story. I believe George Washington was protected from on high, it's obvious God had big plans for him. This story has been authenticated by historians from both the native American and scholars from leading institutions. My question is; "Why hasn't this story been taught in schools?" Aren't we "One Nation under God."

History proves that this "One Nation under God," was indeed founded as a Christian nation. Today, liberals in the news media would like you to believe otherwise. There is just too much proof to dispute the facts. Period. But truth will prevail because there is a rebirth of patriotism in every corner of The United States. I meet thousands of wonderful, believing people who share your passion for truth, justice and the American way of life. The momentum has begun to build and you can begin to speak out for what is right... because it is! Many try to say this is not a nation of Christian principles. Here is the proof that you will never see on the nightly news or read about in the newspapers because they don't want you to know about it.

In 1775, only a year after the British had invaded the colonies, the United States Congress convened to select one of it's own members to organize all the farmers and militia groups into an army that would go up against the mightiest military force on earth. No one thought we could win a war with Great Britain but they all pledged their lives, their fortunes and their sacred honor. George Washington said on July 9th, 1776, "Every officer and man will endeavor so as to live and act as becomes a Christian soldier, defending the dearest rights and liberties of his country. To the extraordinary character of Patriot, it should be our highest glory to add the more distinguished character of Christian."

These were the words of our first president who believed in his Lord's guidance and protection. Whose devine protection was evident as Indian marksmen clearly proved when bullets ripped through the young Washington's coat, all failing to penetrate or even bruise the skin. Yes, Washington's words to his troops prove Christian character was paramount in his leadership and example. His directives were closely reminiscent of the orders given to the Minutemen by the Provential Congress in 1774, Congress reminded the Minutemen that:

"You are placed by Providence in the post of honor, because it is the post of danger. And while struggling for the noblest objectives–the liberties of your country, the happiness of posterity and the rights of human nature–the eyes not only of North America and the whole British Empire, but of all Europe are upon you. Let us be therefore, altogether solicitous that no disorderly behavior, nothing unbecoming our characters as Americans; as citizens and Christians, be justly chargeable to us."

It is obvious our republic was indeed founded as a Christian nation. It's time we stand up and acknowledge this fact, be proud of it, share it with those around you and defend our heritage whenever somebody tries to say otherwise. When I selected the title, many people asked me, "Do you think it will work? Do people really care about a "Rebirth of Patriotism?" Yes, I do think it will work, and I'll tell you why. People are hungry for it. We who served are sick and tired of those who didn't, always telling us what's wrong with our country! And guess what? THEY are what's wrong with America right now. In my show in Branson I see thousands of veterans every month and they always tell me how they wish their grandkids could grow up feeling the pride we felt when we were young and it was "cool" to be proud of our flag, our nation and our president.

I'll paraphrase from Kevin Costner's movie "Field of Dreams" because it answers the question; "Can we have a successful rebirth of patriotism in America?" The reality is yes, and no. If we do nothing, say nothing and continue to sit on our hands, I believe our great nation is doomed because history proves once a nation abandons God, evil enters and immediately erodes the moral foundation of the society. When it collapses, so does the nation, history proves that to be true. But if enough Believers will passionately standup for God, Family and Country, we will renew our spirits and pass along the legacy of 'good' triumphing over evil. Yes, if we shout loud and clear our patriotic beliefs, people will come to join our noble cause. When millions "log-on" to the truth, truth prevails.

In the movie, remember when Costner's character asked James Earl Jones "IF" people would come to see his baseball field in the middle of Iowa, Jone's character smiled broadly and with the joyful passion he felt for the game replied, "Oh, yes, people will come. They'll come for reasons they can't even fathom. They will turn in your driveway not knowing for sure why they are doing it. They'll arrive at your door as innocent as children, longing for the past. They will sit in seats and watch. It will be as if they dipped themselves in magic waters. The memories will be so thick they'll have to brush them away from their faces. People will come. This game is part of our past. It reminds us of all that once was good and it could be again. People will come. People will most definitely come." 17.

140

It took faith to build that baseball diamond in the middle of the Iowa cornfield. And if you saw the movie you'll remember he did it while his friends, family and community thought he was crazy. Well maybe its time you and I act a little crazy, let's start the tide growing by doing these simple "baby-steps" to renew our patriotic hearts.

As we approach the final pages, I think it appropriate to share a few words from our greatest patriots; George Washington, Abraham Lincoln, Franklin D. Roosevelt, Harry Truman, General Dwight D. Eisenhower, John F. Kennedy, Senator Barry Goldwater, Dr. Martin Luther King and Ronald Reagan. If your favorite statesman or president was omitted, forgive me. The following transcribed quotations are from documents that are historical in fact, taken from the respective Inaugural Address transcripts which are part of the public domain. To make Washington's read easier, I have taken the liberty to change the language from some early documents spoken in "Queen's English" and adopted the verbiage into modern terminology that will be easier to read and comprehend. It is with great hope you will read further. I hope their words "fire you up!" As you read through their words, you'll notice the length expands as we near our current era. I do this for I feel these modern day President's are the ones we saw, heard, and learned from their example. There is a need for all Americans to get excited and take an active part in shaping our future by observing our past. Learn from these great men and strive to become more like them. We are the examples to our families and must live to never embarrass our good name.

The following communications are from presidents and statesmen who were or are passionate patriots. The power of their example stand for themselves for each man will be judged by history and by God Almighty.

George Washington

(paraphrased)

Fellow Citizens of the Senate and the House of Representatives. Among the tribulations of life, no event could have filled me with greater anxiety than that of being asked to take on the qualifications outlined by your order, and received on the Fourteenth day of the present month. On one hand, my Country summoned me, whose voice I can never hear but with reverence and love. From my retreat which I had chosen to live out my final days. My health is not the best, but the magnitude of your request and the trust to which you have given to me, I must answer in the affirmative.

In the important revolution just accomplished by these colonies now referred to as The United States, has given our new nation peace and tranquility but at such a high cost. These reflections and thoughts, arising out of the present crisis, have forced me to set aside my personal ambitions of retirement to take on the burdens of my nation's calling. This, I must do as a *Patriot*.

Lincoln's Gettysburg Address

"Four score and seven years ago, our fathers brought forth upon this continent, a new nation, conceived in liberty, and dedicated to the proposition that all men are created equal."

"Now we are engaged in a great civil war, testing whether that nation or any nation so conceived and so dedicated, can long endure. We are met on a great battlefield of that war. We have come to dedicate a portion of that field, as a final resting-place for those who here gave their lives that that nation might live. It is altogether fitting and proper that we should do this."

"But, in a larger sense, we cannot dedicate — we cannot consecrate — we cannot hallow — this ground. The brave men, living and dead, who struggled here, have consecrated it, far above our poor power to add or detract. The world will little neither note, nor long remember what we say here, but it can never forget what they did here. It is for us the living, rather, to be dedicated here to the unfinished work which they who fought here have thus far so nobly advanced. It is rather for us to be here dedicated to the great task remaining before us — that from these honored dead we take increased devotion to that cause for which they gave the last full measure of devotion — that we here highly resolve that these dead shall not have died in vain — that this nation, under God, shall have a new birth of freedom — and that government of the people, by the people, for the people, shall not perish from the earth."

Franklin D. Roosevelt

"A good society is able to face schemes of world domination and foreign revolutions alike without fear. Since the beginning of our American history we have been engaged in change, in a perpetual, peaceful revolution, a revolution which goes on steadily, quietly, adjusting itself to changing conditions without the concentration camp or the quicklime in the ditch. The world order, which we seek, is the cooperation of free countries, working together in a friendly, civilized society. This nation has placed it's destiny in the hands, heads and hearts of it's millions of free men and women, and its faith in freedom under the guidance of God. Freedom means the supremacy of human rights everywhere. Our support goes to those who struggle to gain those rights and keep them. Our strength is our unity of purpose. To that high concept there can be no end, save victory."

Harry S. Truman

"Mr. Vice President, Mr. Chief Justice, and fellow citizens, I accept with humility the honor the American people have conferred upon me. I accept it with a deep resolve to do all that I can for the welfare of this Nation and for the peace of the world."

"In performing the duties of my office, I need the help and prayers of every one of you. I ask for your encouragement and your support. The tasks we face are difficult, and we can accomplish them only if we work together."

"Each period of our national history has had its special challenges. Those that confront us now are as momentous as any in the past. Today marks the beginning not only of a new administration, but of a period that will be eventful, perhaps decisive, for us and for the world. It may be our lot to experience, and in large measure to bring about, a major turning point in the long history of the human race. The first half of this century has been marked by unprecedented and brutal attacks on the rights of man, and by the two most frightful wars in history. The supreme need of our time is for men to learn to live together in peace and harmony. The peoples of the earth face the future with grave uncertainty, composed almost equally of great hopes and great fears. In this time of doubt, they look to the United States as never before for good will, strength, and wise leadership."

"It is fitting, therefore, that we take this occasion to proclaim to the world the essential principles of the faith by which we live, and to declare our aims to all peoples."

"The American people stand firm in the faith which has inspired this Nation from the beginning. We believe that all men have a right to equal justice under law and equal opportunity to share in the common good. We believe that all men have the right to freedom of thought and expression. We believe that all men are created equal because they are created in the image of God."

"From this faith we will not be moved."

Dwight D. Eisenhower

"My friends, before I begin the expression of those thoughts that I deem appropriate to this moment, would you permit me the privilege of uttering a little private prayer of my own. And I ask that you bow your heads: Almighty God, as we stand here at this moment my future associates in the executive branch of government join me in beseeching that Thou will make full and complete our dedication to the service of the people in this throng, and their fellow citizens everywhere. Give us, we pray, the power to discern clearly right from wrong, and allow all our words and actions to be governed thereby, and by the laws of this land. Especially we pray that our concern shall be for all the people regardless of station, race, or calling. May cooperation be permitted and be the mutual aim of those who, under the concepts of our Constitution, hold to differing political faiths; so that all may work for the good of our beloved country and Thy glory. Amen."
Patriotism means equipped forces and a prepared citizenry. Moral stamina means more energy and more productivity, on the farm and in the factory. Love of liberty means the guarding of every resource that makes freedom possible, from the sanctity of our families and the wealth of our soil to the genius of our scientists. And so each citizen plays an indispensable role. The productivity of our heads, our hands, and our hearts is the source of all the strength we can command, for both the enrichment of our

lives and the winning of the peace. No person, no home, no community can be beyond the reach of this call. We are summoned to act in wisdom and in conscience, to work with industry, to teach with persuasion, to preach with conviction, to weigh our every deed with care and with compassion. For this truth must be clear before us: whatever America hopes to bring to pass in the world must first come to pass in the heart of America. The peace we seek, then, is nothing less than the practice and fulfillment of our whole faith among ourselves and in our dealings with others. This signifies more than the stilling of guns, easing the sorrow of war. More than escape from death, it is a way of life. More than a haven for the weary, it is a hope for the brave. This is the hope that beckons us onward in this century of trial. This is the work that awaits us all, to be done with bravery, with charity, and with prayer to Almighty God."

John F. Kennedy

"We observe today not a victory of party, but a celebration of freedom–symbolizing an end, as well as a beginning–signifying renewal, as well as change. For I have sworn before you and Almighty God the same solemn oath our forefathers prescribed nearly a century and three quarters ago. The world is very different now. For man holds in his mortal hands the power to abolish all forms of human poverty and all forms of human life. And yet the same revolutionary beliefs for which our forebears fought are still at issue around the globe, the belief that the rights of man come not from the generosity of the state, but from the hand of God. We dare not forget today that we are the heirs of that first revolution. Let the word go forth from this time and place, to friend and foe alike, that the torch has been passed to a new generation of Americans, born in this century, tempered by war, disciplined by a hard and bitter peace, proud of our ancient heritage, and unwilling to witness or permit the slow undoing of those human rights to which this Nation has always been committed, and to which we are committed today at home and around the world. Let every nation know, whether it wishes us well or ill, that we shall pay any price, bear any burden, meet any hardship, support any friend, oppose any foe, in order to assure the survival and the success of liberty. So let us begin anew, remembering on both sides that civility is not a sign of weakness, and sincerity is always subject to proof. Let us never negotiate out of fear. But let us never fear to negotiate. Since this country was founded, each generation of Americans has been summoned to give testimony to its national loyalty. The graves of young Americans who answered the call to service surround the globe. Now the trumpet summons us again not as a call to bear arms, though arms we need; not as a call to battle, though embattled we are, but a call to bear the burden of a long twilight struggle, year in and year out, "rejoicing in hope, patient in tribulation," a struggle against the common enemies of man: tyranny, poverty, disease, and war itself. The energy, the faith, the devotion which we bring to this endeavor will light our country and all who serve it and the glow from that fire can truly light the world. And so, my fellow Americans: ask not what your country can do for you, ask what you can do for your country."

Senator Barry Goldwater

"I ask your help, and the help of all Americans, so that an American president can tell Nikita Khruschchev; "You are wrong! Our children will not live under communism— your children will live under freedom!""

These words spoken in the fall of 1964 were scoffed and laughed at by the political foes of the time. Now, so many years later we must tip our hats to the presidential candidate because he was correct in his vision. His early eagle-eyed perceptions led to Ronald Reagan forming like-minded beliefs. Twenty years after Senator Goldwater "shocked" the world with his blatent challenge of the Soviet Empire, we did "tear down that wall" and like dominoes the entire system of totalitarianism began to collapse all over the world.

Dr. Martin Luther King

"So I say to you, my friends, that even though we must face the difficulties of today and tomorrow, I still have a dream. It is a dream deeply rooted in the American dream that one day this nation will rise up and live out the true meaning of its creed - we hold these truths to be self-evident, that all men are created equal. I have a dream that one day on the red hills of Georgia, sons of former slaves and sons of former slave-owners will be able to sit down together at the table of brotherhood."

"I have a dream that one day, even the state of Mississippi, a state sweltering with the heat of injustice, sweltering with the heat of oppression, will be transformed into an oasis of freedom and justice. I have a dream my four little children will one day live in a nation where they will not be judged by the color of their skin but by the content of their character. I have a dream today! I have a dream that one day every valley shall be exalted, every hill and mountain shall be made low, the rough places shall be made plain, and the crooked places shall be made straight and the glory of the Lord will be revealed and all flesh shall see it together. This is our hope. This is the faith that I go back to the South with. With this faith we will be able to hear out of the mountain of despair a stone of hope. With this faith we will be able to transform the jangling discords of our nation into a beautiful symphony of brotherhood. With this faith we will be able to work together, to pray together, to go to jail together, knowing that we will be free one day. This will be the day when all of God's children will be able to sing with new meaning-"my country 'tis of thee; sweet land of liberty; of thee I sing; land where my fathers died, land of the pilgrim's pride; from every mountain side, let freedom ring"-and if America is to be a great nation, this must become true. Let freedom ring from the mighty mountains of New York. Let freedom ring from the heightening Alleghenies of Pennsylvania. Let freedom ring from the snow-capped Rockies of Colorado. Let freedom ring from the curvaceous slopes of California. But not only that. Let freedom ring from the Stone Mountain of Georgia. Let freedom ring from Lookout Mountain of Tennessee. Let freedom ring from every hill and molehill of Mississippi, from every mountainside, let freedom ring. And when we allow freedom to ring, when we let it ring from every village and hamlet, from every state and city, we will be able to speed up that day when all of God's children - black men and white men, Jews and Gentiles, Catholics and Protestants - will be able to join hands and to sing in the words of the old Negro spiritual, "Free at last, free at last; thank God Almighty, we are free at last."

President Ronald Reagan

"There are no words adequate to express my thanks for the great honor that you have bestowed on me. I will do my utmost to be deserving of your trust."

"When the first President, George Washington, placed his hand upon the Bible, he stood less than a single day's journey by horseback from raw, untamed wilderness. There were four million Americans in a union of thirteen States. Today we are sixty times as many in a union of fifty States. We have lighted the world with our inventions, gone to the aid of mankind wherever in the world there was a cry for help, journeyed to the Moon and safely returned. So much has changed. And yet we stand together as we did two centuries ago. When I took this oath four years ago, I did so in a time of economic stress. Voices were raised saying we had to look to our past for the greatness and glory. But we, the present-day Americans, are not given to looking backward. In this blessed land, there is always a better tomorrow. Four years ago, I spoke to you of a new beginning and we have accomplished that. But in another sense, our new beginning is a continuation of that beginning created two centuries ago when, for the first time in history, government, the people said, was not our master, it is our servant; its only power that which we the people allow it to have. That system has never failed us, but, for a time, we failed the system. We asked things of government that government was not equipped to give. We yielded authority to the National Government that properly belonged to States or to local governments or to the people themselves. We allowed taxes and inflation to rob us of our earnings and savings and watched the great industrial machine that had made us the most productive people on earth slow down and the number of unemployed increase. By 1980, we knew it was time to renew our faith, to strive with all our strength toward the ultimate in individual freedom consistent with an orderly society. We believed then and now there are no limits to growth and human progress when men and women are free to follow their dreams. And we were right to believe that. Tax rates have been reduced, inflation cut dramatically, and more people are employed than ever before in our history. We are creating a nation once again vibrant, robust, and alive. But there are many mountains yet to climb. We will not rest until every American enjoys the fullness of freedom, dignity, and opportunity as our birthright. It is our birthright as citizens of this great Republic, and we'll meet this challenge. These will be years when Americans have restored their confidence and tradition of progress; when our values of faith, family, work, and neighborhood were restated for a modern age; when our economy was finally freed from government's grip; when we made sincere efforts at meaningful arms reduction, rebuilding our defenses, our economy, and developing new technologies, and helped preserve

peace in a troubled world; when Americans courageously supported the struggle for liberty, self-government, and free enter-
prise throughout the world, and turned the tide of history away
from totalitarian darkness and into the warm sunlight of human
freedom.   My fellow citizens, our nation is poised for greatness.
We must do what we know is right and do it with all our might.
Let history say of us "These were golden years, when the
American Revolution was reborn, when freedom gained new life,
when America reached for her best."

A Few Remember Whens...

Don't you wish you could go back to the time when...

1. Decisions were made by going "eeny-meeny-miney-mo."
2. Mistakes were corrected by simply exclaiming, "do over!"
3. "Race issue" meant arguing about who ran the fastest.
4. Money issues were handled by whoever was the banker in "Monopoly."
5. Catching fireflies happily occupied an entire evening.
6. It wasn't odd to have two or three "best" friends.
7. Being old, referred to anyone over 20.
8. The net on a tennis court was the perfect height to play volleyball & rules didn't matter.
9. The worst thing you could catch from the opposite sex was cooties.
10. It was magic when dad would "remove" his thumb.
11. It was unbelievable that dodge-ball wasn't an Olympic event.
12. Having a weapon in school, meant being caught with a slingshot.
13. Nobody was prettier than Mom.
14. Dad was the strongest man alive.
15. Scrapes and bruises were kissed and made better.
16. It was a big deal to be tall enough for the "big people" rides at the amusement park.
17. Getting a foot of snow was a dream come true.

18. Abilities were discovered because of a "double-dog-dare."

19. Saturday morning cartoons weren't 30-minute ads for action figures.

20. No shopping trip was complete, unless a new toy was brought home.

21. "Oly-oly-oxen-free" made perfect sense.

22. Spinning around, getting dizzy and falling down was cause for giggles.

23. The worst embarrassment was being picked last for a team.

24. War was a card game.

25. Water balloons were the ultimate weapon.

26. Baseball cards in the spokes transformed any bike into motorcycles.

27. Taking drugs meant orange-flavored chewable Flintstone's vitamins.

28. Ice cream was considered a basic food group.

29. Older siblings were the worst tormentors, but also the fiercest protectors.

I'd like to add a personal thought about baseball;

30. Remember when we played baseball from sunrise to sunset, I'd shout, "I'm Mickey Mantle!" My pals would say, "I'm Willie Mays!" or "I'm Hank Aaron!" When you're a kid you don't notice the color of your heroes skin.

I Remember When...

There was a time back in the early 60s when I had to work week-ends at my parents corner grocery store. The 60s was one of the most dangerous times in our nation's history. The Vietnam war claimed it's victims and we watched our televisions reporting the daily casualty counts. I was about 14 years old when all this began to happen. Race riots were flaring all across the land and it seemed our nation was falling apart at the seams. But when you are a kid, skin color doesn't seem to matter much. Here's a true story that happened one Saturday morning when I was about 16 years old. My family owned a little grocery store in Oak Park, a section of Sacramento that was evolving into a mostly black community.

Like most teenagers, I didn't like working all that much. My step-father, Gerald Radford is an honest, hard working man who felt if you didn't work "hard," high achievment was impossible. "Hard work never hurt anybody!" He always said. So, reluctantly, each Saturday morning, as was my assignment I'd punch the keys on the old cash register at Radford's Market. This one particular Saturday morning a bouncy, happy little black girl came skipping her way up to the check-out counter. "Hi Mikey," she said. I don't remember her name, but I do remember how cute her pig-tails were, it looked like she'd received an electrical shock because they were sticking straight out from both sides of her head. "What can I get you?" I asked. "Well, my mommy sent me down here to get some film for her camera cuz weez havin' a party today!" I could tell she was excited about it because she was aglow with anticipation. I got down on one knee and looked into her big brown eyes and asked, "Do you need black and white film, or do you need colored?" She scratched her head, with a puzzled look on her face. Then, with the sweetest innocence I've ever seen replied, "Well Mikey, I don't think no white folks is comin' to da party, soze you can just give me the colored film!" That little girl touched my heart that day. Oh, I wish the rest of us "adults" could be so blind to the color of a person's skin. The world would surely be a friendlier place.

Final Words

In President Reagan's words, he referred to these times as the "golden years" when the American Revolution was reborn. We sit again with a glorious opportunity before us, a time of renewal but also a time of choices that have been bestowed upon us. Do we choose to follow the path cut by Washington, Jefferson and our Founding Fathers? Do we accept the challenges offered in the great speeches on the previous pages just read, or do we fall victim to apathy. I ask you, do we want to limit governments reach into our pockets and purses, or allow it's claws to dig deeper into our hides just as a monster hungers for ever more flesh? Do we, as free citizens of a sovereign nation wish to limit our freedoms or do we stand tall as passionate patriots and shout, "Don't tread on me!" The choices are clearly marked before us. Our future as a free society is contingent upon recognizing the expanding peril enlarging like a cancer inside the hallowed halls in Washington D. C. There are many politicians, on both side of the aisle, who are driven to make us slaves of a "Big Brother" society. Some preach words of compassion and shared responsibility. Others speak the "words" they "hope" we believe, even though they do not. And so I ask you, do you want to control your life's destiny, or are you comfortable knowing someone else will? It could come to that if we sit by and do nothing. However, I strongly believe we will survive the approaching crisis both morally and ideologically. Our Founding Fathers pledged their lives, their fortunes, their sacred honor because they were fed up paying the British Government for taxation without representation. They eventually lost everything in the revolution. Do you know what the high tax rate was that sent them to war with the world's biggest power? Approximately two percent! Think about that next April 15th! I believe God will continue to bless America, "IF" we turn back to Him. The founders knew the power of God's word and the dynamic miracles of His hand. Their certainty and trust in His laws can be seen in every instrument of freedom they penned. We too must observe God's laws, and preserve what so many gave their lives defending because The United States of America is, "One Nation under God, indivisible with liberty and justice for all."

Here's my "Top-Ten List"

Things we can do to begin a rebirth of patriotism:

#1. Buy an American flag and hang it on your front porch. You'll feel an immediate surge in your heart.

#2. See Mel Gibson's movie, "The Patriot," and Stephen Spielberg's "Saving Private Ryan." These films will teach your family the incredible sacrifices of our founding families and show the bravery of "The Greatest Generation" during World War Two.

#3. Register to vote, and do so in every election. Have a "Voting Day" coffee or brunch and then vote en masse.

#4. Because we were founded as a Christian nation, read the "Left Behind" series by Tim LaHaye and Jerry Jenkins ... because you sure don't want to be!

#5. Teach the children in your family "The Pledge of Allegiance" and the meaning of our patriotic holidays.

#6. Teach also, "The Lord's Prayer" and The Ten Commandments.

#7. Visit your local cemetary and place flowers on a veteran's grave.

#8. Support your local Boy Scouts and Girl Scouts; they teach the old fashioned values. Join General Colin Powell's America's Promise.

165

#9. Take a veteran out to lunch and thank him for his service to our country. You will never forget the experience.

#10. Watch the Fox News Network, especially The O'Reilly Factor. It's the only fair, balanced network that "tells it like it is." Watch, then you decide.

It is always difficult to put the final thoughts on the page, but this I do knowing many of you now have hearts beating with a renewed sense of duty, honor and country. My hope is that you are feeling a "Rebirth of Patriotism," and that when you and I stand before our Lord, he smiles and says to both of us, "Well done, my good and faithful servants."

God Bless You...and God Bless America!

The Bill of Rights

We the People of the United States, in Order to form a more perfect Union, establish Justice, insure domestic Tranquility, provide for the common defense, promote the general Welfare, and secure the Blessings of Liberty to ourselves and our Posterity, do ordain and establish this Constitution for the United States of America.

First Ten Amendments to the Constitution of The United States of America

Amendment I

Congress shall make no law respecting an establishment of religion, or prohibiting the free exercise thereof; or abridging the freedom of speech, or of the press; or the right of the people peaceably to assemble, and to petition the government for a redress of grievances.

Amendment II

A well regulated militia, being necessary to the security of a free state, the right of the people to keep and bear arms, shall not be infringed.

Amendment **III**

No soldier shall, in time of peace be quartered in any house, without the consent of the owner, nor in time of war, but in a manner to be prescribed by law.

Amendment **IV**

The right of the people to be secure in their persons, houses, papers, and effects, against unreasonable searches and seizures, shall not be violated, and no warrants shall issue, but upon probable cause, supported by oath or affirmation, and particularly describing the place to be searched, and the persons or things to be seized.

Amendment **V**

No person shall be held to answer for a capital, or otherwise infamous crime, unless on a presentment or indictment of a grand jury, except in cases arising in the land or naval forces, or in the militia, when in actual service in time of war or public danger; nor shall any person be subject for the same offense to be twice put in jeopardy of life or limb; nor shall be compelled in any criminal case to be a witness against himself, nor be deprived of life, liberty, or property, without due process of law; nor shall private property be taken for public use, without just compensation.

Amendment **VI**

In all criminal prosecutions, the accused shall enjoy the right to a speedy and public trial, by an impartial jury of the state and district wherein the crime shall have been committed, which district shall have been previously ascertained by law, and to be informed of the nature and cause of the accusation; to be confronted with the witnesses against him; to have compulsory process for obtaining witnesses in his favor, and to have the assistance of counsel for his defense.

Amendment **VII**

In suits at common law, where the value in controversy shall exceed twenty dollars, the right of trial by jury shall be preserved, and no fact tried by a jury, shall be otherwise reexamined in any court of the United States, than according to the rules of the common law.

Amendment **VIII**

Excessive bail shall not be required, nor excessive fines imposed, nor cruel and unusual punishments inflicted.

Amendment **IX**

The enumeration in the Constitution, of certain rights, shall not be construed to deny or disparage others retained by the people.

Amendment **X**

The powers not delegated to the United States by the Constitution, nor prohibited by it to the states, are reserved to the states respectively, or to the people.

How to Properly Display
the Flag of The United States

Inauguration Day

Martin Luther King's Birthday, 3rd Monday January

Lincoln's Birthday, Feb. 12

President's Day, 3rd Monday February

Memorial Day, Last Monday May (half staff until noon)

Flag Day, June 14 Independence Day, July 4

Labor Day, 1st Monday September

Columbus Day, 2nd Monday October

Veterans Day, November 11

Election Day

Thanksgiving Day

State Holidays

All Patriotic Occasions

It is the universal custom to display the flag only from sunrise to sunset on buildings and on stationary flagstaffs in the open, but it should not be displayed on days when the weather is inclement. If flown at night, the flag should be illuminated. Always hoist the flag briskly, and lower it ceremoniously.

When flown at half staff, first raise to the peak, then lower to half staff. Before lowering the flag, raise it again to the peak, then lower.

If the flag becomes wet or damp, spread out the flag until dry. Do not fold or roll up when damp.

The flag, is no longer fitting for display, it should be destroyed in a dignified way, preferably by burning privately.

Never should any disrespect be shown the flag of the United States of America.

The flag should never be dipped to any person or thing.

Regimental colors, state flags and organizations or institution flags are dipped as a mark of honor.

Advertising signs should not be fastened to a staff or halyard from which the flag flies.

The flag should never be displayed with the union down except as a sign of dire distress. The flag should never touch anything beneath it or the ground, floors, water or merchandise. Never use the flag as drapery.

Never use the flag as a covering or drape a ceiling.

The flag should never have anything placed or written upon it.

Always display the flag to the right side of any lectern or stage.

When the United States flag flys on the same halyard, no foreign flag shall be above it.

When displayed other than on a staff, it should always have the union uppermost left as seen from the wall.

When displayed over a street, the flag should be displayed with the stripes vertical, and the union to the north on an east/west street, or to the east on a north/south street.

For whom great thanks and credit is given:

1. Powell, Colin — US Army General (ret.)
   Source: Internet.

2. Rogers, Roy — Used by permission of Roy Rogers, Jr.

3. Mrosia, Sister Helen — Sourse: Internet

4. Author: Annonomous

5. Author: Annonomous

6. Author: Annonomous

7. Author: Annonomous

8. Author: Annonomous

9. Scott, Darrell — Transcript Congressal Record.
   Source: Internet

10. Haddock, Doris — Transcript Congressal Record.
    Source: Internet

11. Sinclair, Gordon — Sourse: Internet

12. Gholson, Nick — Times Record News, Wichita, Texas

13. Wright, Joe Rev. — Transcript Kansas State Senate.
    Source: Internet

14. Graham, David C. — Sourse: Dear Abby, June 14, 1999

15. Author Unknown

16. Barton, David — The Bullet Proof Washington,
    WallBuilders Press, 1990

17. Robinson, Phil Alden — "Field of Dreams"
    Universal Studios

A Letter to God

Dear God,

Why weren't You in Columbine High School?

Signed,

A Broken Hearted Kid

God write back:

Dear Broken Hearted,

Your politicians won't allow Me in schools anymore.

Signed,

God